BIG PAPI

AND

THE KIDS

CARL H. JOHNSON

Dedication/Acknowledgments

To my wife, Janice Longfellow, one of the most rabid Red Sox fans and, more importantly fan of baseball in general, who provides me with ideas, input and feedback from a fan's perspective in everything I write.

To my children for their interest in baseball and all that they taught me about the game as I played the roles of coach, fan and proud father as they, and I, grew up with the game a major part of our lives.

To Beatrice Silverstein, my High School English Teacher, to whom I always will be indebted, for her encouragement of my writing and the words she said to me sixty years ago and which I have never forgotten 'You should be a sportswriter.'

To Kate Flora, the award winning mystery writer, whose struggles and perseverance when she began her writing career, I was fortunate to have observed, and which encourage me to keep going when the writing gets tough.

TABLE OF CONTENTS

TABLE OF CONTENTS

CHAPTER 1

INTRODUCTION

The 2014 Boston Red Sox had done something no other team in Major League Baseball history had done. Unfortunately, it was not a First to be proud of. They had finished in last place in 2014 after finishing last in 2012 and winning the World Series in 2013, the year in between the last place finishes.

No other team, since the World Series began in 1903, had ever won a World Series after finishing in last place the previous year and then finished last the following year. In a three year period, they went from Worst to First to Worst making a mockery of their comeback in 2013 when they were acclaimed for going from Worst to First.

With that dubious 'accomplishment' behind them, the Sox really had nowhere to go but up in 2015.

They started the 2015 season with two new acquisitions among their position players. They had signed Free Agents Pablo Sandoval and Hanley Ramirez over the off season.
Sandoval, a third baseman, signed for six years for a total of $105. million. He had spent seven years with the San Francisco Giants, batting .294 with a .465 slugging percentage, had won the World Series MVP Award in 2012 and was a two time All Star at third where he was expected to fill a hole for the Red Sox.

Hanley Ramirez, who had spent nine years in the National League with the Miami Marlins and the Los Angeles Dodgers, was a third baseman/shortstop who had hit .300 with a .500 slugging percentage in the NL. He had been named Rookie of the Year in 2006 and had also won the National League batting title in 2009 when he hit .342. Ramirez was expected to be the every day left fielder, although he had no experience there, but the Sox felt he had the natural ability to make the change. He signed a five year contract giving him $110. million over the five years.

In addition to Ramirez and Sandoval, the Red Sox had acquired an almost completely new starting rotation of experienced pitchers all of whom had shown they had the ability to win at the Major League level but there were no outstanding stars among them.

After trading John Lester, the previous year, Red Sox fans expected that they would pay whatever it took to get him back when he became a Free Agent at the end of the year but that hadn't happened so they had tried to build on what they had left.

Rick Porcello, a 26 year old, right handed starter, had been signed as a Free Agent with a five year deal worth $95. million. He had been with the Tigers for six years, winning 10 or more games every year and had won 76 and lost 63 with a 4.30 ERA.

Justin Masterson, a 30 year old, right hander, who had been with the Sox, for a year, at the beginning of his career, had been signed as a Free Agent for $9.5 million for the year. In seven years in the Big Leagues, with the Red Sox, Cardinals and Indians, he had won 10 or more three times and had a career record of 60-72 with a 4.24 ERA.

Wade Miley, 28, a left hander, had been acquired in a trade with the Arizona Diamondbacks. The Sox had given pitchers Rubby De La Rosa and Allen Webster for him. In his four years at Arizona, he had won 10 or more twice and had a record of 58 wins and 59 losses with a 4.34 ERA. He would get $3.7 million in 2015.

The Sox had acquired Joe Kelly, 26, a right hander, and Allen Craig, from St. Louis in trade for John Lackey and Corey Littrell and cash in mid season of 2014. In two years plus at St. Louis, Kelly had won 17 and lost 14, including one 10 win season. His ERA with the Cardinals had been 3.25 and he would be paid just $523,000. for the year.

Clay Buchholz, a 30 year old, right hander, in his ninth year with the team, despite his tendency to injury which had kept him from ever having a complete season, was also planned on as a starter. He had won 66 and lost 44 with the Sox and had a 3.92 ERA.

With this five as starters and the other additions to the roster, fans and management in Boston felt that this team could turn it around and contend. NESN, the Red Sox baseball television network, in their analysis of the Red Sox pitching before the season started, had this to say;

' While it is reasonable to be concerned about the Red Sox rotation given the number of question marks, it's also important to assess the unit based on its context. No team in the American League East has a dominant starting five. The Red Sox offense figures to be much better and Boston's ground ball tendencies are a good fit for Fenway Park.

Would Boston be better off with a legitimate No. 1 starter? Absolutely. Any team would be. But can the Red Sox win with the current group? Sure they can.'

So, what did the Red Sox do in 2015? They won 71 and lost 91, fell into last place on June 9 and stayed there for almost the rest of the season, finishing there, 15 games out of first. Except for a brief period when Torey Lovullo took over as Manager when John Farrell was ill, they looked like, and were, one of the worst teams in baseball.

The two big offensive pickups were flops. Sandoval hit .245 and had only 10 homers and 47 RBI's with an anemic .366 slugging percentage. Ramirez hit .249 with 19 homers and 53 RBI's and was probably the worst left fielder in baseball.

The starters never did get started. Masterson had a 5.61 ERA with just 4 wins and 2 losses and spent quite a bit of time trying to get his act together at Portland and Pawtucket. Miley was 11-11 with a 4.46 ERA. Kelly was 10-6 but had an ERA of 4.82.

Buchholz, as usual had limited duty due to injury, making just 18 starts and winning seven and losing seven. Porcello was 9-15 with a 4.92 ERA.

They had a team batting average of .265, fifth best in the league and scored a fourth best 748 runs. Their team ERA was 4.31, 25th in all of baseball, their pitching gave up 753 runs, the 28th worst in baseball, and gave up more hits, 1,486, than all but four other teams in baseball.

The year had been a total disaster, coming on the heels of the previous last place finish. John Farrell, in five years as a Manager, between Toronto and Boston, had finished last twice in a row, won the World Series, and then finished last twice again. In the five years, his teams had won 400 and lost 410 and, in the last two years, the Sox were 149-175 under him.

On August 18, 2015, with the Red Sox in last place and going nowhere fast, Dave Dombrowski was appointed President of Baseball Operations and General Manager, replacing Ben Cherrington. Dombrowski had rebuilt the Florida Marlins when John Henry, the current Red Sox Owner, was an Owner there and had done the same with the Detroit Tigers. He had a reputation as a Take Charge manager who got things done.

After two of the worst seasons in recent memory, Sox fans expected that their new President would work a miracle and bring them a contender but no one was optimistic that it would happen soon at the end of the 2015 season.

CHAPTER 2

STRENGTHENING THE 2016 TEAM

The ink wasn't even dry on the last articles about the Red Sox season when the Sox announced, on October 4, that John Farrell would return to manage the team in 2016, subject to his health being okay and allowing him to undergo the rigors of the season. Torey Lovullo, who had managed the team so successfully during Farrell's absence while undergoing treatment would return as Bench Coach.

On November 3, the Sox exercised their option and brought back Clay Buchholz for the 2016 season. There was much speculation that that he was just being brought back to use as trade bait. He had missed much of 2015 after suffering a strained right elbow flexor muscle on June 10 and had not pitched again, making only 18 starts, with a 7-7 record and a 3.26 ERA and had a history of long periods on the disabled list.

On November 13, they acquired Craig Kimbrel, 27, a 6", 210 pound, hard throwing right handed Closer, in a trade with the San Diego Padres, in exchange for four prospects.

The Sox gave up Logan Allen, an 18 year old, left handed right fielder who had been playing Low A ball, Javier Guerra a 20 year old, left handed hitting shortstop who had been playing A ball, Carlos Asuaje, a right handed hitting second baseman, who had been at AA Portland and Manuel Margot, a 21 year old, right handed hitting center fielder, who had also been at Portland.

Kimbrel, who had 39 saves in 43 attempts with a 2.54 ERA in San Diego would be paid $11.2 million in 2016, $13.2 million in 2017 and $13. million in 2018, would not be eligible for Free Agency until after the 2018 season and there was a club option for $13. million for the next year. He was with Atlanta before going to the Padres and, from 2011-2014, had 185 saves in 204 attempts with a 1.43 ERA and a 15-10 record.

On November 18, David Ortiz and the team announced that 2015 would be his last season as he would retire at the end of the season. The announcement, made on his 40th birthday, came as a surprise after he had hit .273 with 37 homers and 108 RBI's with a slugging percentage of .553 and hit his 500th homer during the 2015 season. Ortiz cited the physical difficulty he had preparing for and staying in shape for a long season as key to his decision to call it quits.

On December 3, Chris Young, a right handed hitting Free Agent outfielder, was signed to a two year contract. Young, 32, an 11 year veteran with a career .232 batting average, had hit .252 with 14 homers and 42 RBI's with the Yankees in 2015 and was signed to a contract under which he would receive $6.5 million per year and be a Free Agent in 2018.

The next day, all the speculation about whether the Red Sox would sign a Free Agent Ace to lead their pitching staff ended with the announcement that David Price, winner of the Cy Young Award with Tampa Bay In 2012, had been signed to a huge contract. Price agreed to a seven year contract which would pay him $217. million over that period, an average of $31. million a year.

He had started the 2015 season with Detroit, where he had been 9-4 with a 2.53 ERA and was traded to the Toronto Blue Jays at the trading deadline, July 30. With Toronto, he had won nine and lost just one with a 2.30 and was key to the Blue Jays winning the American League East. Critics were quick to point to the fact that Price had a reputation of not being a Big Game pitcher, with a 2-7 record in the post season and a 5.12 ERA in 63 1/3 innings. In 2015, after he helped Toronto get to the Playoffs, he was 1-2 with a 6.18 ERA in the post season.

In 2012, when he won the Cy Young, he had been 20-5 with a 2.56 ERA and, in his nine year career, he was 104-56 with a 3.09 ERA and 1,372 strikeouts in 1,442 innings pitched.

With the Ace they had wanted now on board, the Sox next attempted to strengthen their bullpen, sending Jonathan Aro and Wade Miley to the Seattle Mariners in exchange for Carson Smith and Roenis Elias. Smith, a 26 year old, 6'6", 215 pound, right hander, appeared in 70 games for Seattle, in 2015, his first full year in the Big Leagues. He had struck out 92 batters in 70 innings and had a 2.31 ERA. He would be paid $529,000. for the year and would not be arbitration eligible until 2018 and not eligible for Free Agency until 2021.

Elias, a 27 year old left handed starter, was 5-8 in 20 starts with Seattle last year with a 4.14 ERA. In two years and 49 starts there he had won 15 and lost 20 with a 3.97 ERA.

With these new players in the fold, Dave Dombrowski and the entire Red Sox organization and their fans seemed to settle back to wait for Spring Training to begin.

CHAPTER 3

SPRING TRAINING

The biggest news at the beginning of Spring Training had to do with Pablo Sandoval showing up overweight and appearing to be out of shape. After a disappointing first year with the Sox, both at bat and in the field, Sandoval was expected to be ready to play when he arrived at Spring Training.

John Farrell made it clear that the third base position was up for grabs and that Travis Shaw would be competing for the position with Sandoval. Shaw had been in 65 games with the team in 2015, batting .270 with 13 homers and 36 RBI's, playing mostly first base but had played eight games at third. Although primarily a first baseman, Shaw had also played 43 games at third at AAA Pawtucket in 2015.

Sandoval did not look good in Spring Training, playing in 19 games and getting just 10 hits in 49 at bats for a .204 average and did not look good in the field either with the extra weight slowing him down. Shortly before the end of Spring Training he complained of a problem with his shoulder and was placed on the 15 day disabled list shortly after the season began.

Shaw, who hit .338 in Spring Training with 22 hits in 65 at bats, would start the season at third.

Hanley Ramirez who, with Sandoval, had been one of the Sox biggest disappointments of 2015, at bat and especially in left field, where he had never played before, worked all spring, learning to play first base, with Brian Butterfield, the Sox infield and third base Coach.

He was expected to start the season there and, despite some minor problems early on, seemed to adapt well to the position and, in contrast to the previous year, when he was trying to play the unfamiliar left field position, seemed to be confident and comfortable at the new position. He also looked better at the plate, more relaxed and confident as he hit .321 with 18 hits in 56 at bats.

After opening the Spring, on February 29th, with the traditional split squad games against Boston College, who they beat 6-0 and Northeastern University who they beat 8-3, the Sox got into regular play with the Twins on March 2nd and 3rd, splitting a two game, home and home series with them.

The success or failure of Spring Training has nothing to do with winning ball games. It is all about getting the team and the individual players ready to compete in the upcoming 162 game season and the second season, the Playoffs, that follow it, which are the real reason you play the season in the first place.

A team's won/loss record in Spring Training has never been a predictor of what that team will do when the real games start. That said, the Red Sox won just 14 and lost 18 in Spring Training.

More importantly, they learned a lot about themselves as a team and as individual parts of that team. For example, it quickly became obvious that the switch from left field to first base was a good move for Hanley Ramirez. Unlike 2015, when he was accused of failing to work at learning to play left field, he was working hard to learn first base with Brian Butterfield. Having been an infielder most of his career, it was obvious that he was more comfortable in the infield.

Travis Shaw quickly showed that he had the ability to adapt to third base and easily beat out Sandoval for the start there.

The pitching, as with most Spring Trainings, developed more slowly with pitchers starting with short periods pitching in games and building up as they stretched their arms out and experimented with new pitches and worked on improving command and control. With pitchers, it is even more difficult to predict success or failure based upon Spring Training than with position players but there were no real surprises in Florida.

What had appeared to be the starting lineup for position players, with the exception of third base, before the team got to Florida seemed pretty well set as the team got ready to go north. Shaw had taken third base away from the now injured Sandoval and the starting lineup and batting order and their production in Spring Training looked like this:

NAME	POS	H/AB	AVG
BETTS	RF	24-68	.353
PEDROIA	2B	17-53	.321
BOGAERTS	SS	16-56	.286
ORTIZ	DH	8-45	.178
RAMIREZ	1B	18-56	.321
SHAW	3B	22-65	.338
HOLT	LF	13-52	.250
SWIHART	C	11-44	.250
BRADLEY	CF	20-53	.377

Other players expected to see significant action or make the team in the near future:

YOUNG	OF	10-47	.213
HANIGAN	C	9-28	.321
CASTILLO	OF	11-60	.183
TRAVIS	1B	15-32	.469
MONCADA	IF	1-5	.200
LEON	C	6-22	.273
HERNANDEZ	SS	11-19	.579
MARRERO	OF	9-35	.257
BENINTENDI	OF	3-4	.750

The starting rotation appeared to be David Price, Clay Buchholz, Joe Kelly, Rick Porcello and Steven Wright. Obviously, great things were expected of David Price based on his previous performance and, perhaps more importantly, the amount the Sox had expended to get him.

Buchholz had a 2.84 ERA and looked strong through the spring. Kelly had been a disappointment with a huge, 11.05 ERA, but his strong finish in 2015 gave the team hope. Both he and Porcello, who had a 2.57 ERA in the spring could be expected to do better in their second full year in Boston.

Steven Wright looked like he might fit into the rotation well with his knuckleball. He had been 3-0 with a 2.60 ERA in Spring Training. Of course, no one expected Eduardo Rodriguez to be out long and, based on last year's record, he was expected to fit into the rotation somewhere.

All in all, it looked like a strong unit going north.

CHAPTER 4

THE SEASON OPENS

APRIL 4-10

Opening Day was postponed when the temperature hovered around the freezing mark and the forecast called for steady precipitation through the afternoon. The game was not postponed until about two hours prior to the scheduled start time but it became obvious that they would not get the game in and the decision was made.

Finally, on Tuesday, April 5, the Red Sox played their 116th opening game. The game, played in 33 degree weather, with a wind chill factor of 26 degrees, in Progressive Field, was worth waiting for from the Red Sox perspective.

David Price, the $217 million man, was not bothered by the cold. He went six innings, striking out 10 batters and giving up just five hits and two runs. He gave up four of the hits and two runs in the fourth inning but was in command the rest of the way. Price was pitching in his third straight Opening Day Game with his third different team. He opened for the Tampa Bay Rays in 2014 and for the Detroit Tigers in 2015. He left after six and Tazawa, Uehara and Kimbrel pitched a scoreless inning apiece the rest of the way.

The Sox scored first in the third when Bradley singled and Betts homered to left center. The Indians tied it at 2-2 in the fourth on four singles.

In the top of the sixth Ramirez and Shaw singled and Holt singled to score Ramirez. Shaw the scored on a wild pitch and it was 4-2. The Sox added two in the ninth when Pedroia walked and Ortiz homered to deep right. And the final was 6-2.

After the game, David Ortiz, when asked about his home run coming on the heels of a less than impressive spring, was quoted as saying "When the lights go on, Papi goes on." With Price's 10 strikeouts, Tazawa and Kimbrel's two each and Uehara's one, Sox pitching had 15 strikeouts on Opening Day for the first time since 1913.

Game 2 was played in 59 degree weather with intermittent rain throughout the game. The start of the game was delayed 12 minutes and was only started because the forecast for the next day was more rain so canceling and scheduling a doubleheader Thursday didn't make sense.

Clay Buchholz, who John Farrell named his Number 2 starter, was on the mound for the Sox. After Joe Kelly had had such a great spring and Buchholz had not, most of Red Sox Nation was surprised with the move. The first inning had the fans saying I told you so as Buchholz gave up four runs on a single, double, walk and a two run by Carlos Santana before getting the second out.

The Sox came back with two in the second on a single by Travis Shaw and a homer by Brock Holt but the Indians got another in the last of the second to make it 5-2. Buchholz settled down and got through the third and fourth with no further scoring but left after walking the lead off batter in the fifth, after throwing 94 pitches in four plus innings.

Carlos Carrasco started for the Indians and gave up back to back homers by Ortiz and Ramirez to start the sixth and was relieved by Ross Detwiler, who immediately gave up a pop fly double to Chris Young, batting for Shaw and walked Holt and Swihart to load the bases with no outs. After Bradley drove in Shaw with a sac fly to center, Zach McAllister relieved Detwiler and got Betts on a grounder to third with Holt scoring to make it 6-5 Sox.

In the last of the sixth, Noe Ramirez, who had relieved Buchholz in the fifth, walked the lead off batter, Yan Gomes, who went to third on a single by Marlon Byrd and scored on a sac fly to center by Juan Uribe to tie the score at 6-6. Robbie Ross came in in relief and got out of the inning. In the Sox seventh, with two out, Ramirez singled up the middle, stole second and went to third on a wild pitch but died there when Pablo Sandoval, pinch hitting for Young, flied to center.

In the last of the seventh, Tazawa gave up a one out homer to

Mike Napoli to make it 7-6 Cleveland and that was the scoring for the game as Bryan Shaw shut down the Sox in the eighth and Closer Cody Allen got the Sox 1-2-3 in the ninth for the save. Tazawa took the loss and McAllister got the win.

As expected, Game 3 was postponed by rain and the Red Sox left Cleveland for a three game set with the Blue Jays in the domed Rogers Center in Toronto, beginning Friday. The Jays had split a four game series with the Rays in Tropicana Field to start the season.

After having a great Spring Training, Joe Kelly took the mound in Game 1 for the Sox against Toronto's Ace, 23 year old, Marcus Stroman, who had gone eight innings and beaten the Rays on Opening Day.

Kelly gave up a lead off triple to Kevin Pillar to start the game and when he scored on a sac fly by Edwin Encarnacion, the Sox were down after one for the second game in a row. After Ramirez was thrown out trying to stretch a single into a double with one out in the second, Shaw and Holt hit back to back doubles to tie the score at 1-1. The Sox went up 2-1 in the third when Ortiz doubled to score Bogaerts, who had singled, for his first hit of the year in 10 at bats, to make it 2-1, Sox.

Kelly, who had gotten through the second and third with little trouble, gave up four consecutive singles to start the fourth, then hit Pillar in the helmet with a pitch and last year's MVP, Josh Donaldson hit a grand slam and the Jays were up 7-2 and Kelly was relieved by Noe Ramirez. Ramirez got out of the fourth and pitched a scoreless fifth.

In the sixth, Bogaerts led off with a double and Ortiz walked. After Ramirez grounded out, Shaw walked and Stroman was relieved by Jesse Chavez. Holt greeted him with a line drive grand slam into the short right field corner to make it 7-6, Jays.

The Sox got two in the seventh on singles by Pedroia, Bogaerts, his third hit, Ortiz and Ramirez to go up 8-7. Barnes, Tazawa, Uehara and Ramirez shut the Jays down, with no hits, in the sixth, seventh, eighth and ninth and the Sox won in a great comeback. Kimbrel was impressive in his second appearance and first save, getting Encarnacion, Troy Tulowitzki and Michael Saunders 1-2-3, throwing in the high nineties and keeping the ball down in the strike zone.

The Sox were 2-1 but last year's biggest problem, starting pitching, still looked to be a problem. Rick Porcello was due to start Game 2 against the Jays and the Red Sox were hoping he'd improve on his Spring Training and 2105 performance.

The offense, with 20 runs and double figure hits in each game, including a total of 13 extra base hits and 33 hits in 111 at bats for a .288 batting average, was doing its job but the staring pitching had been terrible for two of the games.

Porcello started for the Sox in Game 2 and, for the third game in a row, the opposition scored in the first inning. Jose Bautista homered to left scoring Donaldson ahead of him and the Sox were down 2-0.

The Sox came back and got three in the top of the third. Rusney Castillo, who started in right in place of Jackie Bradley, singled and a walk to Swihart, followed by an errant pick off throw by Toronto starter R. A. Dickey, moved them to second and third. Pedroia then grounded out, scoring Castillo and Bogaerts and Shaw both doubled to score two more and put the Sox up 3-2.

Shaw started at first, Pablo Sandoval started at third and Ramirez moved to DH to give Ortiz the day off. The lead didn't last long as Bautista homered again with Donaldson on in the last of the third to make it 4-3, Jays.

The Sox tied it in the fourth when Holt struck out but reached first when the third strike got away from the catcher, went to third on Castillo's double to center and scored on a sac fly to center by Swihart. In the fifth, Pedroia singled, Bogaerts walked and Ramirez tripled to right on a ball that took a crazy hop over Bautista's head in right scoring Pedroia and Bogaerts. Ramirez then scored on a passed ball to make it 7-4, Sox.

The Sox added a run in the sixth when Betts singled and Pedroia doubled to right to score him and make it 8-4. Porcello went six innings, giving up the four runs on seven hits and striking out seven. Uehara pitched a perfect seventh and Ross got the Jays in order in the eighth and ninth and the Sox won 8-4.

Porcello got the win and the three hitless innings by Uehara and Ross gave the Red Sox bullpen seven consecutive hitless innings in the last two games.

For the fourth game in a row, the Sox had double figures in hits, with 11 and added six more extra base hits to give them 19 extra base hits in four games. With a 3-1 record, they were in second place, one game behind the Baltimore Orioles, who were 4-0.

The finale in Toronto started just like the last three games. Steven Wright, the Sox starter, gave up singles to Pillar and Donaldson and walked Bautista to load the bases with nobody out in the first. Encarnacion then bounced back to Wright who threw to second for the force but Pedroia's throw to first went wild over Ramirez's head at first and two runs scored. The Sox were down 2-0 after one.

Wright settled down and went 6 2/3 innings, throwing 117 pitches without giving up another run. Unfortunately, the Jays starter, Marco Estrada shut out the Sox for seven innings on just five hits while striking out eight and Storen and Osuna shut them out in the eighth and ninth. Donaldson hit his fourth homer of the year off Noe Ramirez in the eighth and the Jays won 3-0. Osuna struck out the side in the ninth for the save.

The Sox offense, which had been so hot, could manage just seven hits, three of them by Hanley Ramirez who had 10 hits in his first 22 at bats. The only real threat by the Sox came in the third but ended when Pedroia, trying to score from first on a double to right by Bogaerts, was thrown out on a perfect relay from Bautista to Goins to Martin to end the inning.

The Sox headed home for Opening Day at Fenway against the Orioles with a 3-2 record. The Orioles were off to a fast start, having won their first five games and were in first place in the American League East.

CHAPTER 5
THE HOME OPENER
APRIL 11-21

Opening Day at Fen way began with a ceremony honoring David Ortiz on his last Opener in Fen way. Former Boston Greats, Bill Russell of the Celtics, Bobby Orr of the Bruins and Ty Law of the Patriots threw out ceremonial first pitches with Ortiz. Big Pa pi's 15 year old daughter, Alex, surprised her father and the crowd singing the National Anthem before the game.

David Price took the Fen way hill for the first time as a member of the Red Sox and Baltimore rookie center fielder Joey Richard hit his third pitch off the left center field wall on one hop for a double. Price recovered and got the next three batters in order. In the last of the first, Betts, Pedroia, Bogaerts and Ortiz singled in succession and Hanley Ramirez hit a sac fly to center to score Bogaerts with the third run of the inning and the Sox were up 3-0.

After getting seven batters in a row, Price gave up a single, walk and hit batsman to load the bases with one out in the third. Chris Davis singled to center to drive in two runs and Mark Trumbull then hit a long, three run, home run to right center and the Sox were down 5-3.

In the bottom of the fourth, Holt walked, Swihart singled and Bradley hit a little pop fly double down the left field line to score Holt and leave Swihart on third. Betts hit a grounder to short to score Swihart but Bradley attempted to go to third and was thrown out. Pedroia then hit into a double play and the inning ended with the score tied, 5-5. Price lasted five innings and left with the score tied at 5-5 after throwing 103 pitches, striking out eight batters.

Baltimore went up 6-5 when J. J. Hardy and Jonathan Schoop hit back to back doubles in the sixth off Matt Barnes in relief of Price. The Sox came right back to tie it in the last half when Holt, who had reached on a walk again and gone to second on Swihart's second single, scored when Bradley grounded into a force at second but beat the relay throw trying to double him at first.

The game went to the ninth tied 6-6 but Closer Craig Kimbrel, in his first appearance at Fenway as a member of the Red Sox, walked Caleb Joseph and Manny Machado and gave up a monster home run to straight away center by Chris Davis, to put the O's up 9-6.

In the last of the ninth, Mookie Betts hit a lead off homer off Baltimore Closer Zach Britton, Pedroia drew a walk and Bogaerts walked to bring David Ortiz to the plate as the potential winning run. Ortiz grounded into a double play and Britton then struck out Hanley Ramirez and the game was over with the Orioles on top 9-7.

Kimbrel got the loss for the Sox whose record fell to 3-3. Sox pitching struck out 15 Orioles but the two homers by Trumbo and Davis were the difference. Three of the Oriole runners who scored had gotten on base by walks and one as a hit batsman.

Buchholz started Game 2 against the Orioles Dylan Wright. Despite walking Chris Davis and giving up a single to Mark Trumbo in the first, Buchholz got through the inning with no runs. The Sox got two in the last of the first when Pedroia singled and Ortiz homered to deep right on a night when the Sox were giving away a necklace commemorating his 500th homer.

It stayed 2-0 until the fourth when J. J. Hardy hit a two run homer that landed on the top of the right field wall and bounced over to tie the score at 2-2. In the fifth, Bradley singled and scored on a double by Betts, who went to third on a ground out and scored on a wild pitch to make it 4-2, Sox.

Buchholz gave up a single to Davis to lead off the sixth and Trumbo hit a pop behind the plate which Swihart misplayed to give Trumbo a life. Trumbo then homered to make it 4-4. Buchholz walked Wieters and gave up a single to Alvarez and was relieved by Robbie Ross who gave up a sac fly to Hardy to put the O's up 5-4 but then got out of the inning.

In the seventh, Ross gave up a lead off single to Machado and was relieved by Noe Ramirez. After striking out Davis, Ramirez gave up a double to Trumbo, a single to Wieters and another two run homer to Hardy and it was 9-4.

The Sox got one in the eighth when Bogaerts singled and scored on Ortiz's double but that was all the scoring as the Sox lost 9-5. The Sox offense had another game with double figures in hits and had now scored 40 runs, in the first seven games, 5.7 per game, but they had given up 41 and they had lost three in a row to slip to 3-4.

Fans were beginning to grumble as Shaw, who had won the third base job, had been pinch hit for by Chris Young four times in seven games and, aside from one weak pop fly that fell for a double, Young had struck out, popped out and flied out. Young is 1-8 on the year, the only hit that pop fly double, and Shaw is 6-20.

Joe Kelly started for the Sox in the third game against Baltimore, hoping to salvage one win. After walking the first batter, he got through the first inning with no runs. In the second, he gave up a lead off double to Hardy who was thrown out trying to stretch it to a triple on a relay from Betts to Pedroia to Shaw. Despite two walks and a single after that, the O's didn't score. In the third, a double by Machado and a homer by Davis put the Orioles up 2-0.

The Sox tied it in their half of the third when Betts and Pedroia had singles to start the inning and both scored on Bogaerts' double. In the fourth, Holt walked and Bradley tripled off the wall in right to score him. Bradley then scored when Betts grounded out to make it 4-2.

Kelly lasted five innings and left ahead 4-2. Barnes, Tommy Layne, Tazawa and Uehara held the O's scoreless through the eighth and Kimbrel struck out Rickard, Machado and Davis in order in the ninth for the save as the Sox won to even their record at 4-4. Kelly got the win for the Sox, although he gave up seven hits and five walks in just five innings. The Sox got eight hits and Betts and Bogaerts each had two.

The Sox announced that Pablo Sandoval had been placed on the 15 day disabled list with a problem with his shoulder. Red Sox sources said that they did not know when the injury had occurred and Sandoval said that he woke up and could not use his arm. Media reports indicated that he may have been given an ultimatum to lose weight as a condition of playing.

Amid much mystery about Sandoval's status, including rumors that he had been scheduled for an MRI to determine the trouble with his shoulder and also that there had been no MRI because the Sox were happy to have a reason to put him on the disabled list, the Sox made some other roster moves.

Christian Vazquez, who had been rehabbing in Pawtucket coming back from Tommy John Surgery after being injured in Spring Training last year, was brought up to Boston and Blake Swihart, who had been doing the bulk of the catching, was sent down. The Sox announced that Swihart would be given time in left field to learn that position and expand his potential value to the team.

They also optioned Rusney Castillo, who had not been playing at all, to Pawtucket and brought up infielder Marco Hernandez.

In Game 1 against Toronto, the Sox got three in the first on a single by Bogaerts and a double by Ortiz, scoring him and, after Ramirez reached on a passed ball on his third strike, Shaw doubled to score them both. Encarnacion led off the second for Toronto with a homer off Porcello to make it 3-1. After Porcello hit the next batter, Tulowitzki, he struck out Smoak and then, when he struck out Saunders swinging for the second out, Vazquez picked Tulowitzki off first for the third out.

In the bottom of the second, Vazquez, in his first at bat back from surgery, doubled off the left field wall and scored on Betts' single. In the last of the sixth, Pedroia singled to drive in Vazquez, who had gotten his second hit, a single off the wall, and put the Sox up 5-1.

Porcello, who had given up just the one hit to Encarnacion, through six innings, while striking out six, walked Bautista to lead off the seventh and then gave up another homer to Encarnacion to make it 5-3. After striking out Tulowitzki, he was relieved by Tazawa, who got the next two in order to end the seventh. Uehara pitched a perfect eighth and Kimbrel, despite giving up a single and walk held the Jays scoreless in the ninth for his third save and a 5-3 Red Sox win.

David Price started Game 2 against the Jays and gave up a triple to Donaldson followed by a double to Bautista in the first and the

Sox were down 1-0 after one. Bradley led off the Boston third with an infield single and, after Pedroia singled, Bogaerts hit his first homer of the season to put the Sox up, 3-1. Ramirez then doubled to right and Shaw drove him in with his second single of the game to make it 4-1. The Jays made it 4-2 when Bautista singled and scored on an Encarnacion double in the fourth.

Price went seven innings, giving up just the two runs on six hits and striking out nine and left ahead 4-2. Uehara got the Jays without a run in their eighth and Kimbrel struck out Bautista, Encarnacion and Tulowitzki in order in the ninth for his second save in as many days, making him four for four. Price got the win to go to 2-0 and Uehara made his seventh appearance in ten games without giving up a run. He has thrown seven innings and given up just two hits since taking over as set up man for Kimbrel.

The win brought the Sox to 6-4 and put them alone in second place, two games behind Baltimore and two ahead of third place Toronto.

Steven Wright started against the Jays in Game 3 on Sunday for the second Sunday in a row and, like last Sunday, gave up two runs in the first inning and settled down after that and left after six with the score 2-1. Bautista hit a solo homer in the first with two outs and, Encarnacion's grounder to third hit the bag for a fluke hit instead of the third out, singles by Tulowitzki and Colabello made it 2-0.

The Sox got one back in the fifth when Marco Hernandez, playing his first big league game in place of Pedroia, singled to left for the Sox first hit off Aaron Sanchez. Hernandez stole second, went to third on an errant throw and scored on Betts' single.

The Sox would not get another hit until the ninth. They went into the ninth down 5-1 after Layne, Noe Ramirez and Barnes each gave up a run in relief of Wright. Hanley Ramirez led off the ninth with a single off Toronto Closer Roberts Osuna and Shaw homered to deep right to make it 5-3 with no outs.

Osuna, a right hander, then struck out the right handed hitting Young, who Farrell allowed to hit for himself despite the fact that he had struck out twice already and left hander Brock Holt was available. Osuna then struck out Bradley and got Hanigan, another right handed batter to line to third for the final out.

Wright got the loss despite another quality start. He had now pitched 12 2/3 innings, given up just three earned runs against perhaps the most potent offense in the league and the Sox have scored just one run for him. Sanchez got the win, going seven innings and giving up just two hits and one run.

Clay Buchholz started Game 4 at 11:00 a. m. on Patriot's Day. He held the Blue Jays scoreless on six hits before being relieved by Junichi Tazawa with two out and no one on in the seventh. Buchholz got the benefit of four ground ball double plays behind him in the first six innings. The Sox ended up with five in the game. Tazawa got the last out in the seventh and the Sox were up 1-0 going to the eighth.

The Sox had scored the lone run of the game in the second when Ramirez hit a ground rule double to right and scored on a double to center by Rutledge, who had started at third in place of Shaw who moved to DH with left hander J. A. Happ on the mound for Toronto. The right handed hitting Chris Young also started in left in place of Holt, a left handed hitter.

In the top of the eighth, Uehara came in to relieve Tazawa and Pillar got an infield single to lead off the inning. He went to third when Rutledge threw wild to first. Smoak, pinch hitting for Carrera, walked and both runners moved up on a passed ball. Saunders then grounded out to short, scoring Pillar to tie the game. Uehara then hit Donaldson with a pitch and walked Bautista to load the bases. Kimbrel came in in relief and struck out Encarnacion for the second out. He then walked Tulowitzki, forcing in the go ahead run and Martin hit a soft liner that fell in right center, scoring two more and it was 4-1.

In the ninth, Drew Storen came on in relief for the Jays with the score still 4-1. Pedroia singled to right, with one out, to extend his hitting streak to ten games and Bogaerts flied to center for the second out.   Shaw then doubled, scoring Pedroia and Ramirez singled up the middle, scoring Shaw and it was 4-3 with the tying run on first. Farrell sent Ortiz up to hit for Young and he took a called third strike to end the game as the Sox comeback fell short, 4-3.

Uehara got the loss and Happ got his second win of the season for Toronto. Buchholz, despite getting no decision, had his most successful outing of the season to date.

Noe Ramirez was optioned to Pawtucket before Tuesday's opener with Tampa Bay at Fenway and Heath Hembree was recalled to Boston.

Joe Kelly started for the Sox against Drew Smyly for Tampa Bay in Game 1 of their series. Kelly walked two of the first three batters and obviously was having a problem with velocity with his first few fast balls under 90 miles an hour. After it became obvious there was something wrong with his right shoulder, he was removed with two outs and two on. He was later reported to have an impingement in his right shoulder which he had had a problem with in September of last year.

Heath Hembree replaced him and got out of the inning. Just back from Pawtucket hours earlier, he held the Rays scoreless through the fourth. He was replaced by Robbie Ross who gave up just one hit and no runs through the seventh. Tazawa struck out the side with a walk in the eighth and Kimbrel held the Rays scoreless in the ninth.

Unfortunately, while this was going on, Smyly was holding the Sox to one hit through eight, getting them in order in every inning but the third, while striking out 11. He gave up a single to Bradley and two walks in the third but that was it. In the eighth, Erasmo Ramirez got the Sox in order and the game went to the ninth, 0-0.

Matt Barnes came in for the Sox in the top half and gave up a lead off home run to Kevin Kiermaier and, after getting one out, gave up a double to Logan Forsythe. He got the second out but then walked Longoria intentionally and Tommy Layne was brought in to pitch to left hander Corey Dickerson. Brandon Guyer pinch hit for Dickerson and reached when Shaw bobbled his grounder, which should have been the third out, loading the bases. Desmond Jennings then hit a pop fly that fell in short right and bounced into the stands for a ground rule double and it was 3-0.

Alex Colome got Boston in order in the last of the tenth and the Sox, who had suddenly become punchless, were a game under .500. In the first few games, when the starting pitching was terrible, they had hit the cover off the ball. Now, with the starting pitching looking great, they suddenly could not hit. Both teams had 14 strikeouts in the game. Barnes got the loss and Ramirez the win for the Rays, his third with no losses. Boston used seven pitchers in the game after using five the day before and the bull pen would be hurting for Game 2 against the Rays on Wednesday.

The Sox got off to a quick start against the Tampa Bay Ace, Chris Archer, in the first inning of Game 2, when Betts walked, Pedroia singled up the middle and Bogaerts singled to score Betts. Ortiz then hit a long double to center to score Pedroia and Bogaerts and Archer settled down and got out of the inning. In the second inning, Bradley doubled to center and Betts homered to make it 5-0. Boston added a run in the fifth when Bogaerts singled and Ortiz drove him in with his second double of the game.

The Rays came back with two in the sixth when Forsythe tripled and scored on Longoria's ground out. Dickerson then homered to make it 6-2. The Sox got the run back in the last of the sixth when Betts singled, stole second, went to third on a wild pitch and scored on Young's single to left, to make it 7-2.

In the Rays seventh, Kiermaier doubled and scored on a single by Conger to make it 7-3. Tazawa pitched a scoreless eighth in relief of Porcello and Noe Ramirez a scoreless ninth and the Sox won, 7-3. Porcello, who gave up three runs on six hits, with nine strikeouts in seven innings, got his third win, without a loss, despite a 4.66 ERA, while Archer got his fourth loss with no wins for the Rays. More importantly, Porcello gave the bull pen a break with his seven innings of effective work.

With Ace David Price on the mound, the Sox were hoping to win the third game of the series. Price gave up a run in the first when Steve Pearce singled in Forsythe to make it 1-0. The Sox came back with five in the second when Betts singled and Pedroia hit his first homer of the year. Bogaerts doubled, Ramirez singled and Shaw doubled, scoring Bogaerts. Holt then singled, scoring Ramirez. Shaw and Holt then pulled a double steal with Shaw scoring and it was 5-1.

Longoria hit a solo homer in the third to make it 5-2. In the fourth, Kiermaier walked and Casali homered. Forsythe singled and Guyer was hit by a pitch again. Longoria then doubled and when Holt misplayed the ball in left both runners scored. Jennings then doubled to score Longoria and Barnes replaced Price on the mound for Boston. Souza singled to drive in Jennings and the Rays were up 8-5.

The Sox got two back in the sixth when Betts homered to drive in Vazquez, who had walked. They tied it in the seventh when Ortiz and Shaw doubled but Bradley struck out with the bases loaded to leave it 8-8.

In the Rays eighth, Souza doubled in Jennings with William Cuevas on the mound for the Sox to make it 9-8. Cuevas was just brought up from Pawtucket the day before where he had a 1-1 record and a 6.17 ERA in just two starts. Cuevas gave up a double to Kevin Kiermaier to start the ninth and Casali sacrificed Kiermaier to third. Noe Ramirez then replaced Cuevas and Forsythe singled to score the run. Ramirez then hit Guyer with a pitch, the third time he was hit in the game, and Dickerson doubled to score both runners and it was 12-8.

In the last of the ninth, Rutledge, hitting for Holt, doubled, and Young, hitting for Bradley, walked, to put men on first and second with one out but Betts and Pedroia flied out and the Sox lost 12-8. Cuevas got the loss and Price, despite giving up eight runs in 3 2/3 innings got no decision.

The loss dropped the Sox into a tie for third with Tampa Bay at 7-8, 3 ½ games behind 10-4 Baltimore in first place. Pedroia got his 1,500[th] hit during the game and became only the tenth hitter in Red Sox history to reach that number.

CHAPTER 6
TAKING THE LEAD
APRIL 22-MAY 1

The Sox traveled to Houston where they would begin a three game series in Minute Maid Park with the Astros who, despite making it to the playoffs last year, were off to a 5-11 start this year and were in last place in the Western Division.

Boston got off to a good start in Game 1, scoring two in the first when Betts led off with a triple and scored on a single by Pedroia. After two walks loaded the bases, Ramirez hit a sac fly to left, which narrowly missed being a grand slam, to score Pedroia with the second run. They got another in the second on back to back doubles by Bradley and Betts and one in the third on three consecutive singles by Ramirez, Shaw and Holt. In the fourth, with one out, Betts got his third hit of the game, a single to right and scored on a double by Bogaerts, to make it 5-0.

Steven Wright, starting his third game of the season, held the Astros scoreless for six innings before walking three batters and giving up one run in the seventh. Heath Hembree relieved him and got out of the inning and pitched a scoreless eighth. The Sox added a run when Betts got his second triple and fourth hit to lead off the ninth and scored on a wild pitch, to make it 6-1.

Robbie Ross came on in the ninth and gave up two hits, a walk and a run before being relieved by Kimbrel with two outs and two men on. Kimbrel got a ground out to end the game at 6-2 and got his fifth save. Wright, who had now pitched 19 1/3 innings with a 1.40 ERA, finally got a win, making him 1-2. The Sox had 15 hits and moved into second place, 2 ½ games behind Baltimore with an 8-8 record.

Game 2 against the Astros started out on a good note. Betts led off with a single to left and went to second when a pickoff attempt went wild. Betts jammed his finger sliding back into first but stayed in the game. Pedroia then walked and Ortiz singled to right to score Betts. Mike Fiers, pitching for Houston, then struck out Ramirez and Shaw and got Holt on a grounder to first and all the Sox got was one run. Buchholz started for Boston and gave up a single and double in the last of the second to tie it at 1-1.

Buchholz had 1-2-3 innings in the third and fourth but loaded the bases with a walk, hit batsman and single with two outs in the fifth. With a 3-2 count, Colby Rasmus then homered deep to right to put the Astros up 5-1. It was the first grand slam Buchholz had ever given up.

Pedroia doubled to lead off the sixth and, after Ramirez walked and Shaw singled to load the bases with one out, Holt hit a sac fly to left to make it 5-2 but Young grounded to third to end the inning. In the top of the eighth, Rutledge, hitting for Young, doubled to drive in Ortiz who had singled and put the tying runs on second and third with two outs but Bradley flied to right to end the inning 5-3.

With the score 5-3 and Tazawa and Uehara both available in the bull pen, Farrell elected to stay with Roenis Elias, who had come on in the last of the seventh, going into the eighth. He gave up back to back doubles to Gonzalez and Valbuena to start the inning and, after getting one out, gave up another double to Altuve to make it 7-3. After getting the second out, Correa was walked to get to Rasmus, who had hit the grand slam earlier, and he got the fourth double of the inning to make it 8-3. That was it as the Sox went down 1-2-3 in the ninth against Josh Fields.

Elias was making his major league debut and had started only two games in Pawtucket prior to being recalled the previous day. He had lasted just 9 1/3 innings in those two games, giving up seven runs, four earned, and walked seven batters. The intentional walk to Correa, who was 0-2 in the game, in the eighth inning, to get to Rasmus, the cleanup hitter, even with the lefty on lefty advantage, was also puzzling.

The Sox dropped under .500 again and fell into third place behind Toronto, 3 ½ games behind the first place Orioles.

In the finale against Houston, the Sox scored in the first inning for the fifth game in a row, getting three against right hander Scott Feldman. Betts led off with a ground ball single to right against the shift and Pedroia doubled down the left field line. After

Bogaerts grounded out, Ortiz was walked to load the bases. Ramircz then grounded into a fielder's choice but, when Altuve failed to touch second on the pivot, the bases stayed loaded and Betts scored. Shaw was then walked to force in Pedroia and Holt hit a sacrifice fly to center and it was 3-0.

Henry Owens, making his first start of the season, gave up a solo homer to Gonzalez in the second to make it 3-1. The Sox came right back with two in the third on back to back doubles by Hanigan and Bradley and an error by shortstop Carlos Correa and it was 5-1, Sox.

The Astros got two more off Owens in the third on a double by Stringer, two walks, Owens' third and fourth walks, a sac fly and a single to make it 5-3. When Owens gave up a one out single to Altuve in the fourth, he was replaced by Matt Barnes. Owens had looked good at Pawtucket prior to being called up with a 1.00 ERA but had had 10 walks in 18 innings and the control problems continued.

It stayed 5-3 until the last of the ninth when Craig Kimbrel gave up a double to Correa and a homer to Rasmus, his seventh of the year, to tie the game. It was Kimbrel's first blown save in six tries and sent the game to extra innings.

In the top of the twelfth, Ramirez and Shaw singled and Holt sacrificed them to second and third. Hanigan walked to load the bases and Bradley singled to drive in Ramirez with the go ahead run. After Betts hit a ground ball forcing Shaw out at the plate, Hanigan scored on a wild pitch to make it 7-5.

In the last of the twelfth, Hembree, who had pitched a scoreless tenth and eleventh, had men on first and third with one out after a Shaw error and a single but struck out Gattis and Gonzalez to end the game, 7-5. Hembree got the win and had now pitched seven scoreless innings in three games since being brought up. Tazawa pitched 1 2/3 scoreless innings and had now pitched 8 2/3 innings in 10 games with only one run scored against him.

Pedroia had three hits for the Sox and Betts, Ortiz, Ramirez, Hanigan and Bradley all had two hits as the Sox got 16 hits but left 13 runners on base. They moved into a tie for second with

Toronto, 2 ½ games behind the Orioles and traveled to Atlanta for a two game series against the Braves.

For the first time in six games, the Sox did not score in the first inning of Game 1 against the Braves. Rick Porcello and Julio Teheran hooked up in a pitchers' duel that had both teams scoreless at the end of six innings. Each pitcher had given up just three hits and no runner had reached third base.

In the top of the seventh, with one out, Jackie Bradley hit a homer to right to put the Sox up 1-0. The Sox then loaded the bases when Vazquez doubled and Porcello was safe after his attempted squeeze bunt fell between Teheran and catcher A. J. Pierzynski for a single. After Pedroia walked, Bogaerts lined out to right to end the inning with three men on.

In the last of the seventh, after one out, Francouer doubled and Freeman walked. Robbie Ross replaced Porcello and got the next two batters to end the threat, striking out pinch hitter, Eric Aybar, for the last out.

The Sox didn't score again and Uehara held the Braves scoreless in the eighth despite giving up a walk. Kimbrel, after blowing his first save of the year the previous night, came in for the ninth and got the Braves in order, striking out two, for his sixth save as the Sox won 1-0.

Porcello got the win, making him 4-0 for the season, lasting 6 1/3 innings and pitching six or more innings for the 12th time in a row, the most in the major leagues. In the streak, which started August 26 of 2015, he had given up 30 earned runs in 83 innings for a 3.25 ERA and had won eight and lost four.

It was the second night in a row that Bradley had knocked in the winning run and the win moved the Sox to within 1 ½ games of the Division leading Orioles. The Sox had scored more runs, 91, than any other team in the American League and given up more runs, 90, than any team in the League except the Astros.

In Game 2 at Atlanta, the Sox got off to a fast start, getting four runs in the first inning off Atlanta starter Matt Wiser. With one out, Pedroia walked and Bogaerts singled. Shaw, batting cleanup with Ortiz out of the lineup due to there being no DH in the National League park, then hit a 418 foot homer to right to make it 3-0. After Ramirez flied deep to right, Bradley was hit with a pitch and scored all the way from first when Holt hit a bloop double to center to make it 4-0.

Price gave one back on three singles in the last of the first and the Braves got another on two singles and a walk in the fourth to make it 4-2. In the fifth, Pedroia led off with a double, went to third on a fly out by Bogaerts and scored on a wild pitch, to make it 5-2. In the seventh, Betts singled and stole second then scored when Shaw doubled to right and it was 6-2.

After a somewhat rocky start, Price settled down and went eight innings, striking out 14, including eight of the last nine outs, while giving up just the two runs on six hits to lower his ERA to 5.76 from 7.06 where it was after giving up eight runs against Tampa Bay on April 21.

The Sox got five more in the ninth off Ryan Weber with Vazquez, Young, Shaw and Ramirez belting doubles, Bradley tripling and Pedroia getting a single, to make it 11-2. Matt Light made his first appearance on the mound in the Majors for the Sox, in the ninth, in relief of Price. After giving up two singles and a walk to load the bases with no outs, he got the next three batters on ground outs with two runs scoring to make the final 11-4. He had been brought up from Pawtucket on Friday and was throwing in the high nineties but lacked control in the beginning.

In addition to banging out three hits, Bogaerts stole two bases, including a theft of third in the seventh. Price's record went to 3-0 and the Sox third win in a row brought their record to 11-9 and moved them to ½ game behind first place Baltimore, who lost to Tampa Bay for their third loss in a row.

Back in Fenway for the second half of their four game, home and home series, the Sox got off to a quick start against the Braves, scoring two in the first when Pedroia singled and was forced at second by Bogaerts who scored when Ortiz doubled to right. Ramirez then singled up the middle to score Ortiz. After the Braves got one back in the second, Hanigan singled to start the

Sox half, Bradley walked and Betts singled to load the bases. Pedroia then hit a grand slam to right to make it 6-1. The braves got one back in the third after a throwing error by Sox pitcher David Wright loaded the bases. Wright then hit Pierzynski to force in a run and make it 6-2.

Boston got two more in the fourth when Bogaerts walked and Ortiz hit a fly ball double off the top of the wall in left center scoring him. The play was reviewed for a possible homer but the call stayed and Ortiz had his third double in four innings. Shaw then tripled to right to score Ortiz and it was 8-2. Freeman homered off reliever Layne in the eighth and Pedroia got his second home run in the eighth to make it 9-3. The Braves got another in the ninth but the final was 9-4, Sox.

After a rocky start, Wright had another good outing, going seven innings and giving up just one earned run on three hits and striking out eight to improve his record to 2-2 and his ERA to 1.37. The Sox 11 hits included three doubles, one triple and two homers. They remained ½ game back as Baltimore beat Tampa Bay, 3-1.

Buchholz started the final game against the Braves. Boston scored in the first when Pedroia doubled, Bogaerts walked and Ramirez singled to score Pedroia, making it 1-0. The Braves came back with two in the top of the second when Peterson walked, Aybar singled, Smith doubled to score one and Markakis singled, driving in two to make it 3-1, Atlanta. The Sox got one back in the last of the third on doubles by Bogaerts and Ramirez. Markakis drove in another run for Atlanta with a single in the fourth and it was 4-2.

Smith drove in Peterson with a single in the sixth and it stayed 5-2 until the ninth. In the last of the ninth, with two outs, Betts singled, went to second on defensive indifference and scored on a single by Pedroia to make it 5-3 with Bogaerts coming up as the potential tying run. He grounded to short and Pedroia was forced at second for the last out.

Buchholz lasted 6 1/3 innings, giving up five runs on eight hits and got the loss, making him 0-3 on the year. The loss left the

Sox at 12-10, 1 ½ games behind the Orioles.

The Yankees came in for a three game set starting Friday night, April 29th.

In Game 1, Henry Owens made his second start of the year against Masahiro Tanaka for the Yankees. The Yankees scored first when Alex Rodriguez led off the second with a homer. They got another in the fifth after Owens hit Gregorius with a pitch, Ellsbury singled and Gardner drove in Gregorius with a single to right to make it 2-0.

Owens left after six, behind 2-0, after giving up both runs on six hits and three walks. The Sox finally got to Tanaka in the seventh with singles by Shaw and Holt and a two run double off the wall in left by Bradley to tie it.

In the eighth, with Dellin Betances on the mound for the Yankees, Bogaerts singled and Ortiz hit his 507th homer over the left field wall to make it 4-2, Sox.

Barnes and Uehara held the Yankees scoreless in the seventh and eighth and Kimbrel shut them down in the ninth for his seventh save. Uehara got the win, making him 1-1 on the year. The home runs by Rodriguez and Ortiz marked the first time in baseball history two players, over 40, on opposing teams had homered in the same game.

Pat Light was optioned to Pawtucket before Saturday's game and infielder Marco Hernandez was brought up to Boston.

Rick Porcello started Game 2 against the Yankees Michael Pineda. The Sox got two in the second on a single by Vazquez and back to back doubles by Bradley and Betts to go up 2-0. That would be all the runs they needed as Porcello shut out the Yanks for seven on five hits and Ross and Tazawa held them scoreless in the eighth and ninth.

In the Boston sixth, Bradley tripled to drive in Holt, who had walked, and Betts singled to plate Bradley. Ortiz led off the seventh with his second homer in two days, his 508th. Ramirez then walked, Shaw singled and Brock Holt hit a bouncer up the middle which Yankee second baseman Starlin Castro couldn't handle and Ramirez scored. Castro was originally charged with an error on the play but the scorer later changed it to a hit giving Holt the RBI. Bradley then got his second triple in two innings to score Shaw and Holt. That made it 8-0 and that was the final.

Porcello got his fifth win against no losses and lowered his ERA to 2.76. He did not record his fifth win in 2015 until July 8 and, at the end of April last year, his ERA was 5.34. The Orioles lost to the White Sox and the Red Sox moved to just ½ game behind them alone in second place.

On Sunday afternoon, before the Red Sox-Yankees game that night, Baltimore lost to the Chicago White Sox, 7-1, as Chris Sale got his sixth win for the ChiSox and the Red Sox moved into a tie for first place with the Orioles with a chance to claim sole possession of first place for the first time since April 22 of 2015.

David Price was less than impressive in the first five innings of Game 3 against the Yankees, giving up three runs in the third on a homer by Alex Rodriguez with two men on and three in the fifth when he hit Ellsbury with a pitch, walked Gardner and gave up a double to Rodriguez and a single to Teixeira.

The Sox got one in the first on singles by Betts and Pedroia and a fielder's choice by Bogaerts which scored Betts. They got three in the third on singles by Pedroia, Bogaerts, Ramirez and Holt and a walk to Ortiz to go up 4-3.

After the Yankees went up 6-4 in the fifth, Ortiz singled to lead off the Sox fifth and was forced at second on a Ramirez grounder to third. Shaw then homered to right to make it tie it at 6-6. It was Shaw's third homer of the year.

After giving up the Yankees six runs, Price got the last eight batters he faced in order before leaving after seven, tied 6-6. In the last of the seventh, with the score still tied, and Holt on first and two out, the Yankees brought in Betances to relieve Nova, who had relieved starter Eovaldi. Christian Vazquez hit Betance's first pitch over the Green Monster and onto Lansdowne Street for his first homer of the year and gave the Sox an 8-6 lead. It was the second homer of Vazquez's career.

Uehara came in for Price in the eighth and gave up a run on a double by Castro and a run scoring wild pitch, to make it 8-7 and it stayed that way into the top of the ninth. Kimbrel came in to close the ninth and got the Yankees 1-2-3, striking out Gregorius and Gardner for his eighth save. Price got the win, despite the rocky start, making him 4-0 on the season.

The Sox moved into sole possession of first place, by one half game, and, after a day off on Monday, traveled to Chicago for a three game series with the White Sox who, with a record of 18-8, led the Central Division by three games. Since Chris Sale had pitched his sixth victory on Sunday, Boston would be spared batting against him in this series.

With the sweep by the Red Sox, the Yankees fell to 8-15 with their fifth loss in a row and were mired in last place, six games out of first.

CHAPTER 7
BACK TO SECOND PLACE
MAY 2-8

Steven Wright started his fifth game of the season in Game 1 at the White Sox. For the fifth time, he went more than six innings, this time giving up just two runs on three hits. He gave up one in the first on a single by Eaton and a triple to Abreau and another in the third when he walked two batters and issued an intentional walk to Abreau to load the bases with one out. Frazier then grounded to third, scoring Jackson to make it 2-0. He settled down after that and gave up only one more hit, a single, through the sixth.

Unfortunately for Wright, the White Sox starter, left hander, Jose Quintana silenced the Sox bats, giving up just four hits in eight innings, one of them a solo homer to right by Hanley Ramirez in the fifth to make it 2-1.

Carson Smith, just off the disabled list, made his first appearance in relief of Wright and pitched a perfect inning in the seventh. Tazawa came on in the eighth and gave up two more runs making it 4-1 going to the ninth and Chicago Closer David Robertson got the Sox 1-2-3 in the ninth. It was Robertson's ninth save of the young season and the surprising White Sox record went to 19-8 and Quintana got his fourth win against one loss.

Wright, who has deserved better support, saw his record slip to 2-3. With a 1.67 ERA and five quality starts, the Red Sox, who lead the league in runs scored with 135, had scored just 10 runs in his starts. With the loss, the Sox slipped into second place, ½ game behind Baltimore, with a 15-11 record.

Clay Buchholz started Game 2 at Chicago and gave up a two run homer to right by Jose Abreau, his fourth, in the last of the first and it looked like Buchholz was on his way to another bad game. However, after giving up a walk and a single in the second, he got Austin Jackson to hit into a double play to end the inning and settled down. He went seven innings, giving up just one more walk and no more hits and holding the ChiSox scoreless the next five innings.

Boston got one back in the third on singles by Vazquez, Bradley and Bogaerts and took the lead, 3-2, on Ortiz sixth homer of the year, with Bogaerts aboard, in the fifth. They got another in the seventh on singles by Betts, Bogaerts and Ortiz. It was Bogaerts' third hit of the game. In the eighth, Young doubled, went to third on a ground out and scored on Rutledge's single to make it 5-2.

Uehara pitched a 1-2-3 eighth and Kimbrel earned his ninth save with a scoreless ninth, despite giving up a walk to Abreau. Buchholz got his first win against three losses.

While the first place Red Sox were playing the first place White Sox on the south side of Chicago, in Game 3 on Thursday night, the Cubs, in first place in the NL Central, were playing the Eastern Division first place Nationals on the north side of Chicago. It marked the first time in MLB history that four first place teams were playing in the same city on the same day.

With one out in the first of Game 3, Pedroia hit Chicago starter Erik Johnson's first pitch over the left field wall for a homer, putting the Red Sox up 1-0. It was the 10th game in the last 15 that they had scored in the first inning. Chicago got it right back in the last half when Adam Eaton singled to right, went to second when Rollins walked, stole third and scored on a ground ball double play.

In the second, Holt singled and scored on Hanigan's double to left. Boston loaded the bases with one out but couldn't score again as Bogaerts lined out and Ortiz grounded to third. They left five runners on in the first two innings. Ramirez homered to right to lead off the third and Shaw tripled into the gap in right center. Holt then hit a sac fly to center, scoring Shaw, and it was 4-1, Boston.

Avisail Garcia led off the fourth with a homer and Hembree replaced Owens who had walked six batters in three innings. Chicago got one more in the fifth when singles by Cabrera, Lawrie and Garcia loaded the bases and Hembree walked Sanchez to force in the run. Barnes replaced Hembree and got Jackson to fly out to Betts in right. When Lawrie tried to score from third, Betts made a perfect throw to the plate to get him for the third out. Chicago appealed the call at the plate but the replay upheld the call and it stayed 5-3, Boston.

Tazawa replaced Barnes in the seventh and struck out the side while allowing a single. In the eighth, Bradley and Betts walked to lead off the inning and moved to second and third on Pedroia's ground out to second. Bogaerts flied out to center and Bradley scored. Ortiz then doubled to center, scoring Betts and it was 7-3, Boston.

Robbie Ross pitched the eighth and ninth, holding Chicago scoreless and striking out three, while giving up just one walk and the Sox won 7-3. Barnes got the win to make him 2-1. The Red Sox were now 17-11, having won eight of their last ten and remained in first place, one half game ahead of Baltimore who beat the Yankees 1-0.

They now left for a three game series in New York with the Yankees, who had lost eight of their last 10 games, had a record of 9-17 and were in last place in the East, 4 ½ games out of first.

Rick Porcello, 5-0, started Game 1 of the Yankee series against Michael Pineda, 1-3. The Sox scored in the first inning for the 11th time in 16 games, getting two when, with two out, Bogaerts doubled down the right field line and Ortiz followed with a long homer to right center, his 50th career homer against the Yankees and his seventh of the year.

The Yankees got one back in the last of the first when Ellsbury walked to lead off, stole second and third and scored when McCann doubled to right. Ellsbury had to leave the game at the start of the second with a strained right hip, apparently incurred while stealing third.

They got another to tie the score in the second. Castro reached on an infield single, was sacrificed to second by Aaron Hicks, who had moved to center from right when Ellsbury left, and scored on a single to center by right fielder Dustin Ackley, batting in Ellsbury's spot.

It was tied at 2-2 until the last of the seventh when Hicks hit a lead off homer to right center making it 3-2, New York. In the eighth the Sox had runners on first and second with two outs and Andrew Miller struck out Jackie Bradley to end the inning.

In the ninth, the Sox loaded the bases on an infield single by Rutledge and singles by Pedroia and Betts but Miller struck out Ortiz on a called third strike after Manager Farrell had been ejected for arguing the second strike. After the called third strike, Ortiz had to be restrained and he was ejected as well. Hanley Ramirez came up with the bases loaded and two outs and he struck out swinging and the Sox had lost the game 3-2.

They squandered 13 hits, leaving 12 runners on base. Travis Shaw had three hits and Porcello went seven innings, giving up just the three runs on six hits for his first loss.

The Orioles game was rained out so the Red Sox, at 17-12 were tied with the O's, who were 16-11, in first place but the Sox trailed by percentage points .593 to .586.

David Price started Saturday's Game 2 against the Yankees' Nathan Eovaldi. Price got through the first and second unscored on and the Sox got one in the top of the third when Ramirez was hit by a pitch, went to second on a ground out and scored on Holt's single to left. In the third, Headley singled, was sacrificed to second by Gregorius and scored on a double to center by catcher Austin Romine and it was 1-1.

In the Yankee third, Castro singled, Teixeira reached on an infield single off Shaw's glove and Ackley walked to load the bases. Gregorius then doubled to right to empty the bases and the Yankees were up 4-1. Jackie Bradley homered to right center with no one on in the Boston fifth and it was 4-2.

The Yankees got two in the fifth on a double to left by Beltran scoring Hicks and Castro, who had both walked. Barnes relieved Price after the double and got out of the inning but it was now 6-2, New York. Hicks hit a sac fly to drive in the seventh run in the sixth and Romine doubled in another in the Yankee eighth and it was 8-2, the final score.

Price went 4 2/3 innings, giving up six runs, making him 4-1 and raising his ERA to 6.75. Baltimore split a doubleheader with Oakland putting them one half game up on the second place Sox.

Steven Wright started Game 3 against the Yankees and the Sox got two in the first inning when Pedroia homered over the short fence in right field, driving in Betts, who had led off with a walk, ahead of him. It was the 12th game of the last 18 that Boston had scored in the first inning.

Wright held the Yankees scoreless for eight innings until giving up a two out, solo homer to Brett Gardner in the ninth. He threw only 101 pitches, 66 of them strikes, while walking just one and striking out seven to gain his third victory and lowering his ERA to 1.52, fourth best among starters in baseball.

The Sox got solo homers from Ortiz in the fourth and seventh, his eighth and ninth of the season, giving him 512 for his career, and Bogaerts, his second, in the eighth to give them a 5-1 win. The win kept them in second, ½ game behind the Orioles who beat the Athletics 11-3. Jackie Bradley had a single and double as he extended his hitting streak to 14 consecutive games and Hanley Ramirez went hitless, ending his 11 game streak. Ortiz had now hit 453 home runs as a member of the Red Sox and moved ahead of Carl Yastrzemski into second on the Sox all time list behind Ted Williams who hit 521 as a member of the Red Sox.

The Sox returned home after the game to face the Athletics in a three game series.

CHAPTER 8
HOME AGAIN
MAY 8-15

Clay Buchholz started Game 1 against Oakland's Ace, Sonny Gray. After pitching well his last time out, Buchholz gave up a run in the first after walking the lead off hitter Coco Crisp, giving up a single to Brett Lawrie moving Crisp to third and got Josh Reddick on a ground out with Crisp scoring. The first three batters were all former Red Sox players. The A's got two more in the second on two singles and a double to make it 3-0.

The Sox got one back in the second on a double by Shaw who went to second on a ground out and scored on a wild pitch to make it 3-1. Khris Davis hit a solo homer for Oakland in the third to make it 4-1.

The Sox chased Gray in the fourth inning, scoring six and sending 11 batters to the plate. They had four doubles in the inning, one each by Shaw and Betts and two, in the same inning, by Ortiz. Holt had a two run homer driving in Shaw, who had reached on his third hit of the game, in the fifth, to make it 9-4. In the sixth, with two out and the bases loaded, Jackie Bradley hit a grand slam to deep right and it was 13-4.

Buchholz had gotten through the fourth and fifth with no further scoring but was removed after five innings. The A's got one unearned run off Carson Smith in the seventh when Bradley misplayed a ball allowing the run to score.

In the last of the seventh, with Rutledge on third after a walk, a wild pitch and a long fly out, Ortiz hit a high pop in front of the plate and the A's let it drop for a single and Rutledge scored to make it 14-5. The A's got two in the ninth on two doubles and a single off Hembree, who pitched the eighth and ninth, to make the final score 14-7.

Buchholz got the win, making him 2-3 on the season, with a 5.90 ERA and the Sox upped their record to 19-13, tied for first place with Baltimore but behind .600 to .594 in won loss percentage. The Blue Jays and Rays were three games back, tied for third.

In Game 2 against the A's, Boston started Sean O'Sullivan who had been in one game in relief against the Yankees since being brought up from Pawtucket. He is a right hander with seven years big league experience. The Sox had signed him as a Free Agent from Philadelphia in December and he had been 2-2 in five starts at Pawtucket with a 3.00 ERA. He had been with the Los Angeles Angels, Kansas City Royals, San Diego Padres and the Philadelphia Phillies and had compiled a 12-23 record and a 5.96 ERA in his seven seasons in the majors.

The Sox continued their first inning hitting getting three runs on a lead off homer by Betts and a two run homer by Ramirez that traveled 468 feet over the left field wall. They added five in the third with doubles by Pedroia and Shaw and four singles to knock out A's starter Sean Manaea. Shaw added a three run homer in the fifth and they got two more in the seventh on a hit batter, two singles and an error by third baseman Yonder Alonso.

O'Sullivan held the A's scoreless for five despite giving up seven hits. In the sixth, he gave up four runs on five hits, including two wall ball doubles to make it 11-4. Robbie Ross relieved him in the seventh and gave up another run to make it 11-5 and the Sox got two in the last of the seventh to make the final 13-5.

Tazawa and Kimbrel pitched the eighth and ninth without any more scoring. O'Sullivan, despite giving up four runs and 12 hits, didn't walk a batter and got his first win with the Sox. Bradley had two hits to stretch his hit streak to 16 games and also threw out a runner at the plate in the second inning. Ramirez, Young and Shaw had three hits apiece and Shaw drove in five runs with a double, homer and single.

The Sox had 16 hits and remained tied for first place with Baltimore who beat Minnesota 5-3. The Sox moved to seven games over .500 for the first time since 2013.

In Game 3, with Rick Porcello starting for the Sox, the A's got one in the second on a single by Vogt and a double by Alonso. The Sox came back with three in the last half of the inning on a double by Young, Shaw was hit by a pitch and Bradley hit a homer to right to make it 3-1.

The A's got two to tie it in the third when Khris Davis singled with runners on second and third. In the last of the third, Pedroia and Ortiz walked and, with two out, Young got his second double to drive in Pedroia and put the Sox up 4-3. In the fourth, Betts singled and Pedroia homered and it was 6-3.

Bradley doubled after Shaw and Vazquez had singled in the fifth to score Shaw and Vazquez then scored on a ground out by Betts. After Bogaerts singled and Ortiz walked to load the bases, Ramirez doubled to drive in two more and it was 10-3. In the sixth, Betts singled in Vazquez, who had doubled and Bradley got his second homer of the game and sixth of the year, with Vazquez aboard in the ninth to make the final 13-3.

Porcello, despite his poor start, gave up just three runs on six hits in 6 2/3 innings for his sixth win with just one loss. Layne, Uehara and Barnes finished up in relief of Porcello, allowing no more runs. The Sox had 17 more hits, giving them 48 hits in the three game sweep against the A's. They scored 40 runs in the three games and gave up just 15. Their team batting average was at .293, the highest in baseball.

Bradley, with two homers and a double, extended his hitting streak to 17 games. They had five starters with batting averages over .300, Pedroia .306, Bogaerts .328, Ortiz .322, Ramirez .313, Shaw .323 and Bradley .322. It was the first time in Red Sox history that the team had scored 13 or more runs in three consecutive games.

The struggling Houston Astros were coming in for a three game series with their Ace, last year's Cy Young winner, Dallas Keuchel, matched up against David Price who had been having problems with command and velocity but thought he had resolved them by a minor adjustment.

The Sox got to Keuchel in the first inning when Pedroia singled and Bogaerts hit a homer to deep left to make it 2-0. It was the 13th time this year the Sox had scored multiple runs in the first inning. Price had struck out the side in the first after giving up two singles to start the game. In the second, despite giving up an earned run on a single, double and error, he struck out the side again.

That was all the scoring for the Astros as Price held them to six hits while striking out 12. His velocity and command were much improved, he was consistently around 94-95 miles per hour. The Sox got 11 runs on 14 hits to give them 51 runs on 62 hits in the last four games.

Ramirez had three hits, Betts had a three run homer and they had four doubles including the 599th of David Ortiz' career. Bradley extended his hitting streak to 18 games and Price got his fifth win against one loss. Tazawa got the last out of the seventh in relief of Price and Hembree pitched a 1-2-3 ninth to close out the 11-1 win.

Baltimore came from behind to beat the Tigers, 7-5, on a five run seventh inning capped by a two run triple by second baseman Jonathan Schoop to keep the O's in a tie for first with the Red Sox.

In Game 2, on Friday, the 13th of May, Houston got a single run in the first, off starter Steven Wright, on singles by Altuve, his first of three hits, Rasmus and Gonzalez. The Sox got five in the second. A single by Ramirez and walks to Shaw and Holt loaded the bases and Hanigan doubled into the triangle in center driving in two and Bradley doubled to right to score Holt and leave Hanigan at third. Hanigan then scored on a wild pitch and Betts singled in Bradley and it was 5-1 Boston.

In the fifth, Wright gave up a double to Castro, an infield hit to Merisnik and a run scoring single by Altuve. Springer then got a double, his second of three hits to score two more and Gonzalez singled in the fourth run to make it 5-5. In the top of the sixth, Springer homered, off his UConn college teammate, Matt Barnes, with Castro on base to make it 7-5, Houston.

Shaw hit his fifth homer, a solo shot in the last of the sixth to make it 7-6 but that was all the scoring as the Sox lost. Houston reliever Harris and Closer Gregerson held the Sox scoreless in the eighth and ninth, striking out five batters between them.

Barnes took the loss for the Sox making him 2-2. Feldman got the win and Gregerson got his eighth save. Jackie Bradley got three hits upping his hitting streak to 19 games and his average to .341. Baltimore shut out Detroit, 1-0, behind Chris Tillman to go one game up on the Red Sox.

Clay Buchholz started Game 3 for the Sox and gave up a solo home run to Astro short stop Carlos Correa in the first inning. The Sox got two in the bottom of the first on singles by Betts and Bradley, who had been moved into the second spot in the lineup with Pedroia being given the day off, followed by a ground rule double by Bogaerts, scoring Betts. After Ortiz walked to load the bases and Ramirez grounded to third forcing Bradley out at the plate, Shaw walked to force in Bogaerts putting the Sox up 2-1.

In the second, Buchholz loaded the bases on a single and two walks and Springer hit his second home run in two days, a grand slam, to make it 5-2, Houston. Ortiz homered with no one on in the Boston third to make it 5-3. In the fourth, Rutledge doubled to left, went to third on Vazquez' single to left and scored as Betts' grounded to third, forcing Vazquez at second, making it 5-4.

In the ninth, with one out, Bradley walked and was forced at second when Bogaerts grounded to second. With two out, Ortiz hit a long triple into the triangle in center to score Bogaerts to tie the game. With Ortiz on third with the potential game winning run and two outs, Ramirez attempted to bunt and was thrown out at first ending the inning.

The game went to the last of the eleventh still tied 5-5 as Smith, Layne, Tazawa, Kimbrel and Uehara held the Astros scoreless in relief of Buchholz.

With two outs in the last of the eleventh, Bogaerts got his third hit of the game, a single to right. After Bogaerts went to second on a wild pitch, Houston Manager A. J. Hinch elected to continue to pitch to Ortiz even though first base was open. Ortiz then hit a 2-2 change up for a long fly ball double into the triangle to drive in Bogaerts with the winning run.

Ortiz was mobbed by his team mates after the walk off. It was the twentieth walk off of his career and his 600th double making him one of only three people in baseball history to have 600 doubles and 500 home runs. The other two are Hank Aaron and Bobby Bonds. Bradley's first inning single extended his consecutive game hitting streak to 20.

Buchholz had another poor start, giving up five runs on seven hits in six innings and walking three. His ERA was now 6.11 and, with Eduardo Rodriguez and Joe Kelly due back from the disabled list soon, Buchholz's future with the Sox did not look bright.

In Game 4 of the series, Sean O'Sullivan started for the Red Sox against Chris Devenski. Boston started hot again scoring two in the first when Betts and Pedroia walked to start the inning and, when Bogaerts lined out to right, Betts moved to third. Pedroia then stole second and, when the throw went wild, Betts scored. Then, with two out, Ramirez doubled to left to score Pedroia.

After getting the Astros 1-2-3 in the first, O'Sullivan gave up a three run homer to Valbuena in the second. Rasmus, who had reached on an error by O'Sullivan and gone to second on a bad throw by Bogaerts and White, who had walked, scored ahead of Valbuena to put Houston ahead 3-2. In the last of the second, Rutledge doubled, Hanigan singled to drive him in, Betts singled and Bogaerts hit his fourth homer to make it 6-3, Boston.

Correa homered, with no one on, for the Astros in the fourth and it was 6-4. Mike Fiers came in to pitch in the fifth for the Astros and Ramirez and Bradley singled, putting runners on first and third, and Rutledge stole second. Hanigan then singled to left to drive in both and make it 8-4. Valbuena got a ground rule double to right in the fifth to drive in two and cut the Boston lead to 8-6.

In the Houston sixth, Altuve reached on a fielder's choice and stole second and third. With two outs, and Hembree on the hill for Boston, Correa reached on an error by third baseman Rutledge with Altuve scoring. Rasmus then doubled to left scoring Correa and tying the score. White then hit a soft line drive to center for a single, scoring Rasmus with the go ahead run and the Astros were up 9-8.

In the last of the seventh, with Scott Feldman pitching for Houston, Rutledge singled to right. Holt then struck out for the second out and was ejected when he argued the call. Hanigan then hit a routine fly ball to right center that right fielder Springer and center fielder Gomez inexplicably let fall between them and Rutledge scored all the way from first to tie the score. Bogaerts then smashed a triple into the gap in right center, scoring Hanigan with the go ahead run.

Tazawa and Kimbrel then shut down the Astros in the eighth and ninth and the Sox won 10-9, with Kimbrel getting his 10th save. Hembree got the win in relief of O'Sullivan, making him 2-0. O'Sullivan had now given up nine earned runs and 17 hits in 10 1/3 innings in two starts.

Ramirez, in the DH spot in place of Ortiz, had three hits. Rutledge, playing third as Shaw took over first for Ramirez had three hits and scored three runs Hanigan also had three hits, drove in four runs and scored two as the Sox pounded out 14 hits.

On the seven game home stand, they had won six and lost one. They had scored a total of 73 runs and had 101 hits, scoring in double figures in five of the seven games and getting 11 or more hits in every game. Baltimore lost to Detroit putting the Sox in a tie for first again, still percentage points behind Baltimore.

CHAPTER 9

BACK ON TOP

MAY 16-26

They now traveled to Kansas City for a three game series against the Royals in Kauffman Stadium. The Royals had been struggling and were in third place in the Central Division with a record of 18-19.

After a rain out, the Sox got one in the second of Game 1, to go up 1-0 on a single by Shaw and a double by Bradley. Bradley's hit extended his consecutive game hitting streak to 22 games. Red Sox starter Porcello gave up a triple to Orlando and a homer to Hosmer to make it 2-1 in the third. In the fourth, four consecutive singles gave the Royals three more to make it 5-1.

Porcello was removed after giving up a lead off double to Cuthbert in the sixth. It was the first start this season that Porcello had failed to complete six innings. The Sox made it 5-4 in the sixth when Bogaerts singled and, after two were out, Ramirez was hit with a pitch and Shaw homered to deep right center, his sixth homer of the season and third hit of the game.

Red Sox Manager Farrell was ejected from the game in the top of the seventh for arguing a called strike on Mookie Betts. It was Farrell's second ejection of the season.

In the Royals eighth, with one out and catcher Perez on first, Uehara came in in relief and, when Infante bunted to try to sacrifice Perez to second , Uehara threw the ball into right field and Perez scored all the way from first. Orlando then hit a homer to left, driving in Infante. It was number nine hitter Orlando's third hit of the game and gave him four RBI's for the game. That made the score 8-4 and that's how it ended as the Sox could not score again.

Porcello got the loss and his record went to 6-2. It was the 12th straight game that the Sox had scored in the first or second inning. The team batting average entering the game was .295, 20 points higher than the second highest, Colorado, at .275.

The Sox lost an opportunity to move into first place alone as Baltimore lost to Seattle, 10-0. They would play a double header on Wednesday to make up for Monday night's rain out.

Steven Wright started the first game of the double header, Game 2 of the series, for the Red Sox and gave up a two run homer to Hosmer in the first, his second in two days. In the Red Sox fourth, Pedroia doubled and Bogaerts singled to put runners on first and third with no outs. Ortiz singled to drive in Pedroia and leave two men on with no outs but Shaw and Rutledge struck out and Bradley grounded out and the inning ended 2-1.

Chris Young homered to lead off the Boston fifth, his first of the season, and it was tied 2-2. In the sixth, Dyson tripled and scored on a sac fly by Cain and it was 3-2 Royals. In the Red Sox eighth, Bogaerts singled and, when Ortiz singled to right, Bogaerts tried to go to third but was cut down on a perfect throw from right fielder Dyson.

There was no further scoring and the Royals won 3-2. Wright pitched all eight innings for the Sox, giving up three runs on five hits and striking out six and got his fourth loss against three wins despite having a 2.52 ERA, fourth best in the American League. It was his second complete game of the season. Bradley's single in the ninth ran his consecutive game hit streak to 23.

With Ace David Price on the hill against Kansas City's Ian Kennedy, the teams traded solo home runs for five innings of the nightcap. Bradley homered with two outs in the second and Betts led off the Sox third with a homer after doubling in the first to make it 2-0. Royal catcher Perez made it 2-1 with a homer in the fourth. The Sox got two more in the sixth when Vazquez singled with the bases loaded to drive in Shaw and Rutledge.

Boston added a run in the eighth on a walk to Rutledge, a single by Bradley and Rutledge scored when Vazquez grounded to third getting his third RBI of the game and making it 5-1. Escobar doubled with one out in the eighth and Tazawa replaced Price on the mound for the Sox. Cain met him with a single to center, driving in Escobar and making it 5-2. Hosmer then lined to Betts in right and he doubled Cain off first to end the inning.

Kimbrel pitched a scoreless ninth for his 11th save and lowered his ERA to 2.50. Price, who lasted 7 1/3 innings, giving up just two runs on five hits, improved his record to 6-1. Bradley's consecutive game hitting streak was now 24. Bogaerts' batting average was at .339 and he led the American League in hits with 57.

With the split, the Sox fell to ½ game behind Baltimore but the O's lost to Seattle on Thursday while the Red Sox were idle so the Sox moved back into a virtual tie for first, headed home for a three game series with Tito Francona's Indians starting Friday.

Before Friday's game, Brock Holt was placed on the seven day disabled list with concussion like symptoms and Carson Smith went on the 15 day disabled list with soreness in his elbow.

Friday night Clay Buchholz started for the Sox against Corey Kluber for the Indians. Boston got off to a 1-0 lead in the first on a lead off double by Betts, who was sacrificed to third by Pedroia and scored when Bogaerts grounded out. After Ortiz walked and Ramirez singled to load the bases with two out, Shaw popped to short to end the inning. Bradley led off the second with a homer to straight away center, to extend his hitting streak to 25 games and put the Sox up 2-0.

In the top of the third, Cleveland got four on a three run homer by Kipnis and a sac fly by Gomes scoring Lindor, who had doubled, stolen second and went to third when the catcher's throw hit him and went into the outfield.

That was all the scoring for the game and the Indians won 4-2. The Red Sox never really threatened and were held to five hits by Kluber, who went seven innings for his 3rd win. Shaw pitched the eighth and gave up a single to Pedroia and Cleveland Closer Cody Allen struck out the side in the ninth, around a walk to Bradley, for his 10th save in 10 tries this season. Buchholz picked up his fourth loss against two wins going six innings and giving up three earned runs.

Bogaerts extended his consecutive game hitting streak to 14 with a fifth inning double. The loss dropped the Red Sox back into second place, a game behind Baltimore who beat the Angels 9-4.

Bradley's homer marked the 20th consecutive game in which the Red Sox had homered, a franchise record.

Joe Kelly returning to the hill, after being out since April 19 with an impingement in his right shoulder, had a no hitter going in Game 2 until Juan Uribe hit a double to right center with two outs in the seventh. After the hit, Farrell pulled Kelly, who had thrown 104 pitches, and brought in Junichi Tazawa, who got out of the inning with no score.

The Sox had scored three in the third on singles by Betts, Pedroia, Bogaerts, Ortiz and Ramirez, the last coming with the bases loaded and driving in two runs. Mookie Betts hit a solo homer, his eighth, in the fourth to make it 4-0 and run the Sox streak of games with home runs to 21.

In the Sox seventh, Ramirez beat out a little roller in front of the plate, Shaw doubled and Bradley was intentionally walked to load the bases. After Vazquez forced Ramirez at the plate with a grounder to third, Swihart walked, forcing in Shaw. Betts then hit his second homer of the game, a grand slam, to left and it was 9-0.

With Hembree on the mound for Boston in the ninth, Santana homered for the Indians' sole run and the Sox won 9-1. Bradley had beaten out a grounder to second in the sixth to extend his hitting streak to 26 games. Kelly picked up his second win without a loss and showed no ill effects from his injury.

The Sox remained one game behind Baltimore in second place.

The Red Sox started Porcello in Game 3. In the first, Pedroia walked, Bogaerts singled to left and Ortiz singled to right to score Pedroia. Ramirez hit a shot off the pitcher's glove and Bogaerts scored when Ramirez was safe at first. Cleveland walked the red hot Jackie Bradlcy to load the bases and Shaw and Swihart struck out leaving them stranded.

In the Indian second, with two out, Uribe doubled to center and Davis was hit with a pitch. Santana walked to load the bases and Kipnis drove in two with a single to right to tie the game at 2-2.

The Sox went up 3-2 in the last of the second when Betts and Bogaerts singled and Ortiz hit a ground rule double to right center to score Betts. In the Sox fifth, Ortiz homered to make it 4-2. Jackie Bradley singled to right extending his streak to 27 games but was stranded. In the Sox sixth, Betts doubled to left and Bogaerts hit a pop fly that dropped for a single and Betts scored the final run, making it 5-2 Sox.

Porcello, who went 5 2/3 innings, giving up just two runs on five hits, got his 7th win and Kimbrel, who got the Indians 1-2-3 in the ninth, got his 12th save. Ortiz went 4-4 with three RBI's and his home run in the fifth gave the Sox a streak of 22 games with at least one home run, the longest such streak in Red Sox history.

At the end of the game Bogaerts was hitting .346, Bradley .342, Ortiz .329, Ramirez .315 and Shaw .305.

Baltimore lost to the Angels 10-2 to move the Sox back into a tie for first. They had Monday off with the Colorado Rockies, in third place in the National League West, with a 21-22 record, coming in on Tuesday.

The Sox announced on Monday that reliever Carson Smith would undergo Tommy John surgery and would be out for a least the rest of the season. Smith had only pitched in three games this season but had been expected to be an important part of the bull pen. In Seattle last year, the 26 year old had appeared in 70 games with a 2.31 ERA.

As seemed to be the usual Boston start, they scored two in the first inning of Game 1 against Colorado when Pedroia singled, Bogaerts doubled and Ortiz drove them both in with a single to left against the shift. The Sox had now scored 49 first inning runs in the season compared to their opponents' 15.

Colorado came back with a run off starter David Price in the second on a walk to Ryan Raburn and a triple by Gerardo Parra to make it 2-1. The Sox got two more in the last of the second when Bradley led off with a double high off the left field wall to extend his streak to 28 straight games. Vazquez then tripled him in and scored on a sac fly by Betts to make it 4-1. Center fielder Charlie Blackmon led off the Rockies third with a homer to make it 4-2.

In the Sox fourth, after Pedroia and Bogaerts walked, Ortiz

doubled to right to drive them in, giving him four RBI's for the game and seven in the last two games. Chris Young drove in Ortiz with a single and it was 7-1. In the Rockies' seventh, Carlos Gonzalez tripled and scored to make it 7-3. The Sox added one in the eighth on singles by Betts and Pedroia and Betts scored when third baseman Nolan Arenado could not handle the throw from the outfield trying to get him at third to make the final 8-3.

Price went seven strong innings giving up three runs on five hits and striking out six and winning his seventh game against one loss. Uehara relieved him in the eighth and struck out the side after giving up a single. Barnes pitched the ninth and struck out two of the three batters he faced.

Bogaerts extended his consecutive game hitting streak to 17 and upped his average to .349 with a double and single in four at bats and the Sox got 12 hits giving them 29 games with 10 or more hits of the 45 they had played. For the first time in 23 games they failed to get a home run breaking their streak.

Baltimore lost to Houston and the Red Sox moved into sole possession of first place with the best record in the American League and the second best in all of baseball behind the Chicago Cubs. Their team batting average of .297 was the best in baseball and was 47 points higher than the Major League average of .250. Bogaerts' .349 led the American League in hitting, Bradley was second at .346 and Ortiz fifth at .333.

Steven Wright, with a record of 3-4 despite a 2.52 ERA, started Game 2 for the Red Sox. He gave up a run to the Rockies in the second when Carlos Gonzalez singled to center, went to second on a passed ball and third on a wild pitch and scored on Mark Reynolds' ground out. They got another in the second on a single to left by Gonzalez, who moved to second on a passed ball, to third when Reynolds singled to center and scored on another wild pitch.

Wright's knuckler was moving so much it was almost impossible for Hanigan to catch it. Hanigan left the game after four innings because of stiffness in his neck. The Sox got four in the fourth. Bogaerts led off with a homer over the green monster, Ortiz walked and Ramirez hit a grounder to third and Ortiz was forced at second. Bradley then singled to left to extend his streak to 29 games and Shaw singled to left scoring Ramirez to tie the game. Swihart tripled to right to drive in two and make it 4-2.

Pedroia doubled down the left field line and had to be removed from the game with tenderness in his hamstring. After Bogaerts struck out, Ortiz was intentionally walked. Ramirez then walked to load the bases and Bradley hit into a force play, scoring Hernandez, who had run for Pedroia and Shaw doubled in two more to make it 7-2.

Wright went seven innings, giving up three runs, two earned, on seven hits and was removed after Arenado led off the eighth with a single. Layne relieved him and the Rockies scored on a single by Gonzalez and a ground out by Reynolds. The Sox added three in the eighth when Swihart got his second triple and scored on Betts' single to left. After Hernandez singled to center, Ortiz doubled to left to drive in Betts and Hernandez and make the final 10-3.

Bradley got two hits to raise his average to .350 and Bogaerts' one hit dropped him to .349 and Bradley took over the league lead. Baltimore lost to Houston, 4-3, for their third straight loss and the Sox after four wins in a row now led the Division by two games over the O's.

Going for the sweep in Game 3 against the Rockies, the Sox got two in the last of the first on a single to left by Bogaerts and a homer by Ortiz to right center, his 12th of the year and the 515th of his career.

Buchholz started for the Sox in a game that was crucial to his staying in the rotation. For three innings, he was perfect, getting the first nine batters in order. Blackmon led off the Rockies fourth with a single to left and, after Buchholz got the next two batters, Gonzalez homered to right center to tie the game at 2-2.

In the fifth, Colorado got four on a single by Parra, a homer by Story, a single by Descalso and another homer by number nine hitter Garneau before Buchholz got anybody out, to make it 6-2. After Gonzalez led off the sixth with an infield single, Buchholz was replaced by Heath Hembree who held the Rockies scoreless through the sixth but gave up a single run in the 7th. The Rockies got another in the ninth off Layne in relief of Hembree to make the final 8-2.

Jon Gray started and went 7 1/3 innings for Colorado, giving up just the two runs in the first and improving his record to 2-2. Buchholz took the loss, dropping him to 2-5. Jackie Bradley went 0-4, despite two long fly ball outs caught at the base of the wall, to end his streak. Bogaerts, with his single in the first, increased his consecutive game hit streak to 19.

The Sox stayed two games up on Baltimore, who lost to Houston for their fourth loss in a row. The Sox now left on a trip to Toronto for three and Baltimore for four before coming home to face Toronto for three more.

CHAPTER 10

FACING THE EAST

MAY 27-JUNE 5

Over the next ten days, the Sox would be playing six games with the Blue Jays and four with the Orioles. Given the standings at the start of this period, this could be a crucial part of the season for them, if any period could be called crucial this early in the year.

The Red Sox announced before Friday's game with Toronto that Clay Buchholz had been removed from the starting rotation and would be working out of the bullpen. Eduardo Rodriguez would be activated from the disabled list and would start in Buchholz's spot in Baltimore on Tuesday.

Joe Kelly started the opener in Toronto and gave up a first inning solo homer to third baseman Josh Donaldson. The Sox got the run back in the top of the second when Shaw grounded to short and went to second when the throw to first went wild. He moved to third when Ramirez grounded out and scored on a ground out by Jackie Bradley. The Jays went up 2-1 in the third when Carrera singled and Donaldson doubled to drive him in.

Singles by Bogaerts, Shaw and Ramirez in the top of the fourth tied it at 2-2. Toronto loaded the bases with one out in the bottom of the fourth and Donaldson singled in one run and Encarnacion drove in another with a sac fly and it was 4-2. Smoak hit a solo homer to lead off the Toronto fifth and it was 5-2. After Pillar doubled with two out, Kelly was replaced by Barnes who got out of the fifth.

The Sox made it 5-4 in the seventh on a walk to Ramirez, a single by Bradley and a soft roller to the pitcher by Hernandez moving them to second and third. Vazquez then singled up the middle driving in two. In the top of the eighth, Pedroia led off with a fly ball to left center which center fielder Pillar and left fielder Saunders let drop between them for a double. Pedroia went to third on a fly out and Shaw singled off first baseman Smoak's glove to score Pedroia with the tying run.

Uehara came in to pitch the eighth for Boston and gave up a lead off single to Carrera and a two run homer to Donaldson, his fourth hit, second homer and fourth and fifth RBI's of the game to make it 7-5 Toronto. Blue Jays Closer Osuna got the Sox 1-2-3 in the ninth and the Jays took Game 1.

Uehara got the loss for Boston and Joe Biagini got the win for the Jays. Osuna got his 11th save. Bogaerts hit in his 19th consecutive game. The Red Sox lead over Baltimore dropped to one game as the O's beat Cleveland.

Rick Porcello started Game 2 against the Jays Ace Marcus Stroman. The Jays got first blood in the third on back to back doubles by Barney and Pillar, the eight and nine hitters and, after the bases were loaded, Porcello hit Encarnacion with a pitch forcing in another run to make it 2-0. Saunders hit into a ground ball double play, scoring the third run.

Bogaerts led off the fourth with a homer and Ortiz doubled to left and Ramirez walked. Bradley then hit a liner to short which short stop Barney caught and doubled Ortiz off second to end the rally with the Sox down 3-1. The Sox got four in the fifth on doubles by Vazquez and Pedroia and singles by Betts and Ramirez. Pedroia and Ramirez each drove in two runs with their hits and it was 5-3, Boston.

Bradley led off the sixth with a double and Shaw homered to make it 7-3. In the last of the sixth Blue Jay catcher Russell Martin hit a solo homer and it was 7-4. In the Sox seventh, Bogaerts got his third hit of the game a single to center and went to second when Pillar booted the ball in center. He went to third on a wild pitch and scored when Ramirez singled to center and it was 8-4 Boston.

Tommy Layne came in in relief for the Sox in the eighth and hit Saunders with a pitch. When Smoak reached safely on a debated call on a force play, Tazawa replaced Layne and gave up a single to Martin and a double to Travis to make it 8-7 and after Kimbrel came in and got the second out on a strikeout, Bautista singled to right to tie the game at 8-8.

Ortiz hit a solo homer in the top of the ninth to put the Sox back on top 9-8. In the last of the ninth, Kimbrel got the first two batters out but Smoak singled, stole second and went to third when Vazquez's throw went into center. Martin then doubled to left center for his third hit of the game and scored Smoak, to tie the game again. It was Martin's third RBI of the game. Travis then singled to left center scoring Martin with the winning run and the Sox had lost their third in a row 10-9.

Kimbrel blew his second save and got his second loss. Bogaerts with three hits and three runs scored, raised his average to .351 and extended his hitting streak to 21 games. He also stole second in the fifth and Chris Young's steal of third in the sixth gave the Sox 32 steals in 35 attempts for the season. Bogaerts had three hits in a game for the ninth time this season. It was the 31st game the Sox had had ten or more hits in on the season.

Baltimore lost to Cleveland 11-4 so the Red Sox remained in first place alone, one game ahead of the Orioles.

The two Major League Cy Young Award winners from 2012 faced each other in Game 3. David Price, who won the American League Award with the Tampa Bay Rays, started for the Sox and R. A. Dickey, who won in the National with the New York Mets, began the game for the Blue Jays. They were scoreless until Price gave up a single to Carrera and a two run homer to Bautista with one out in the fifth to put the Jays up 2-0.

Dickey, who had held the Sox hitless for 5 1/3 gave up a triple to Betts with one out in the sixth. Pedroia singled to score Betts and went to second on a single by Bogaerts who extended his consecutive game hitting streak to 22. Shaw walked to load the bases and Dickey hit Ramirez with a pitch to drive in Pedroia with the tying run. Dickey was then relieved by rookie Chad Girodo who walked Bradley to force in another and make it 3-2. Jesse Chavez then relieved Girodo and got the next two Red Sox batters with no further scoring.

It stayed 3-2 until the eighth when Encarnacion tied it with a lead off homer off Hembree, who had relieved Price in the seventh. The game went to the top of the eleventh tied and Swihart and Betts walked with one out. Pedroia then hit a long drive to right center which bounced over the fence for a ground rule double, scoring Swihart with the go ahead run and leaving runners on second and third with one out. Bogaerts then grounded out to short and Betts was able to score to make it 5-3. Uehara came in in the last of the 11th and got the side in order, striking out Bautista and Donaldson for the last two outs.

Buchholz, who had relieved in the tenth and held the Jays scoreless, got the win for Boston in his first relief appearance. Uehara got his first save of the year. Kimbrel was not available to pitch as he had thrown 39 pitches the day before, a high for his career.

The attendance for the three game series in the Rogers Center was 142,490. The win avoided a sweep for the Sox and kept them one game ahead of the Orioles going to Baltimore for a four game series starting Monday.

The following column appeared in the Biddeford Journal Tribune on May 29, 2016.

THE LEGACY OF THEO EPSTEIN

In 2002, Theo Epstein became General Manager of the Boston Red Sox. At age 28, he was the youngest General Manager in baseball history. He had come to the Sox from the San Diego Padres where he had worked under Larry Lucchino in the Public Relations Department. When Lucchino became President and CEO of the Red Sox, he hired Epstein to work for him.

Under Epstein, the Sox broke the Curse of the Babe and won the World Series in 2004 and again in 2007. In 2011, after losing a shot at the Playoffs by losing 20 of their last 27 games, the Red Sox parted ways with Manager Terry Francona and, shortly thereafter, Epstein left to take the position of President of Baseball Operations for the Chicago Cubs.

With Chicago, Epstein built a pennant contender in a short period of time. As of Wednesday of this week, the Cubs were in first place in the Central Division of the National League, with the best record in baseball and five games ahead of the second place Pittsburgh Pirates, after making the playoffs as a Wild Card team last year.

Meanwhile, back in Boston, the Red Sox were in first place in the Eastern Division of the American League with a record of 28-17, the second best record in baseball behind, who else, the Cubs.

In the first third of the season, the Sox have been riding the big bats in their lineup as their starting pitching has been less than spectacular. Six of the starting position players were hitting over .300 with Xander Bogaerts leading the league at .349, Jackie Bradley, second at .346, and David Ortiz fifth at .333, and Ramirez .311, Pedroia .303 and Shaw .301. The starting lineup, with Brock Holt out with concussion like symptoms consists of Christian Vazquez behind the plate, Hanley Ramirez at first, Dustin Pedroia at second, Xander Bogaerts at short and Travis Shaw at third. The outfield has Blake Swihart in left, Jackie Bradley in center and Mookie Betts in right with David Ortiz in the designated hitter slot.

Of these nine position players, eight were acquired during Theo Epstein's time as General Manager and President of Baseball Operations for the Red Sox. The only exception was Hanley Ramirez, who was signed as a Free Agent before the 2015 season.

Ortiz was signed as a Free Agent on January 22, 2003 and Pedroia was drafted by the Sox in the 2004 Amateur Draft. Bogaerts was signed as an Amateur Free Agent in 2009 and Vazquez was drafted in the Amateur Draft in 2008. Amazingly, Betts, Shaw, Bradley and Swihart were all drafted in the 2011 Amateur Draft. Reliever Matt Barnes was also acquired in that draft. Theo and his staff obviously knew what they were doing that year. Also acquired during that draft was Henry Owens, who, if he can regain his control, could eventually be a main part of the starting rotation.

The other position players on the roster, Chris Young was signed as a Free Agent in 2015, Josh Rutledge was acquired in a trade with the Los Angeles Angels in 2015, Ryan Hanigan in a trade with the San Diego Padres in 2014 and Marco Hernandez in a trade with the Chicago Cubs in 2014.

Of the pitchers currently on the 25 man roster only Barnes, Junichi Tazawa, who was acquired as a Free Agent in 2008 and Clay Buchholz who was drafted in 2005 came to the Sox during the Epstein years.

Of the starting pitchers, besides Buchholz, David Price was acquired as a Free Agent this year, Rick Porcello in a trade with the Tigers in 2014, Joe Kelly in a trade with the St. Louis Cardinals in 2014 and Steven Wright in a trade with the Cleveland Indians in 2012.

Of the relievers, with the exception of Barnes and Tazawa, Craig Kimbrel, the Closer, was acquired in a trade with the San Diego Padres in 2015, Robbie Ross in a trade with the Texas Rangers in 2015, and Heath Hembree in a trade with the San Francisco Giants in 2014. Koji Uehara was signed as a Free Agent in 2012 and Tommy Layne as a Free Agent in 2013.

While Theo can't be given credit for the Red Sox pitching in 2016, he left the Sox with a formidable group of position players, most of whom will be around for many years in a Red Sox uniform. While he made his share of errors in the Free Agent market as almost every General Manager in baseball has done, he built an organization by drafting intelligently and developing his prospects within the system.

As for Terry Francona, who left among the controversy over a blown pennant race and a beer and fried chicken scandal that the media blew out of proportion, he is back home in Cleveland where he and his father both spent portions of their major league careers. His Indians are in the middle of their fourth straight winning season after having endured four losing seasons before Francona took over. He has won 281 and lost 247 in four years and is in second place just 2 ½ games out of first in the American League Central Division.

It's very possible that this season could end with the Cubs and the Red Sox playing in the World Series. If they do, no matter who wins, much of the credit for developing the winner should go to Theo Epstein who turned both organizations around and put them on the paths they are now on.

CARL H. JOHNSON
MAY 29, 2016

The Sox now traveled to Baltimore for four games with the second place Orioles, who they led by just one game, in Camden Yard.

Leading off Game 1, on May 30, Mookie Betts singled through the right side against the shift. With the hit and run on, Pedroia grounded out to short and Mookie was safe at second. Bogaerts then hit a little dribbler down the third baseline and the pitcher and catcher went after it and the catcher, Caleb Joseph, threw Bogaerts out at first. Betts never stopped at third and ran right by the catcher and pitcher on the third base line to score from second, standing up, to put the Sox up 1-0. In the third, Betts and Pedroia singled and Bogaerts doubled to score Betts and it was 2-0, Red Sox.

Steven Wright started for the Sox and held the O's to one hit for four innings. In the last of the fifth, he gave up a triple to Nolan Reimold, a double to Ryan Flaherty and a single to Joseph putting runners on first and third with no outs. Adam Jones hit a sac fly to score Flaherty and tie the score, 2-2.

Bradley put the Sox back on top with a solo homer, his ninth, to lead off the sixth and Ortiz led off the eighth with another solo homer. After Ortiz's homer, his 517th, Marco Hernandez, playing third with Shaw at first to give Ramirez a day off, hit his first big league homer with Shaw and Swihart on base to make it 7-2.

That was the final as Wright held the O's hitless for the last four innings to get the complete game win, his third complete game of the year. He gave up just four hits while throwing a career high 122 pitches and improving his record to 5-4 and his ERA to 2.45.

Bogaerts, with two doubles, a walk and two RBI's, increased his league leading average to .354 and Ortiz increased his league leading RBI total to 47.

The Sox bull pen got a valuable day off with three more games coming up in Baltimore followed by three at home against Toronto. The win moved the Red Sox two games ahead of the Orioles.

Eduardo Rodriguez, ERod, made his first start for the team since injuring his knee in Spring Training. Jackie Bradley was absent from the team, taking paternity leave as he and his wife were expecting their first child being born within a day or so. Rusney Castillo was brought up from Pawtucket to fill the vacancy created on the roster.

Before ERod took the mound, Betts and Pedroia gave him a two run lead with back to back lead off homers to greet Oriole starter Kevin Gausman. In the Sox second, with two outs and Young, filling in in center for Bradley, and Swihart on base with walks, Betts hit his second homer in two innings to make it 5-0, Boston.

In the Orioles' third, right fielder Joey Rickard singled and scored on left fielder Nolan Reimold's double to make it 5-1. The O's got another back in the fifth when center fielder Adam Jones singled to score third baseman Paul Janish, who had doubled.

Rodriguez gave up just the two runs on six hits before being relieved by Ross to start the seventh. Betts hit his third homer of the game, a solo shot to right in the seventh to make it 6-2 and it stayed that way as Ross, Uehara and Kimbrel shut the O's down the rest of the way. The three homers gave Betts 12 for the season and the five RBI's raised his total to 40 the highest total among lead off hitters in baseball.

Rodriguez got his first win of the season and the Sox went three games up on Baltimore with the 6-2 win.

Unbelievably. Mookie Betts hit the second pitch of Game 3 for a home run, giving him four homers in six at bats, and putting the Sox up 1-0. The lead would not last long as Joe Kelly gave up singles to Jones and left fielder Hyun Soo Kim and walked Davis to load the bases in the Orioles first. Right fielder Mark Trumbo then singled to score Jones and Kim and catcher Matt Wieters hit a sac fly to left, scoring Davis. DH Pedro Alvarez doubled in Trumbo and it was 4-1, Baltimore.

Shaw led off the second with a double, his 18th, and Young homered to center to make it 4-3 in the Sox second. With two outs, Betts hit a solo homer to center field to tie the game. It was his fifth in two games and he became the first batter in Major

League history to hit home runs in both the first and second inning of consecutive games.

The O's took the lead back on a sac fly by Machado in the last of the second, making it 5-4. In the Sox third, Ortiz hit a solo homer, his 15th, to right field. Shaw singled and Swihart and Young walked to load the bases. Hanigan then singled to center, scoring Shaw and Swihart and Betts was walked to load the bases. Pedroia grounded out to end the top of the third with the score 7-5, Boston.

In the last of the third, Alvarez singled and scored on a double by Schoop and Tommy Layne relieved Kelly for the Sox. Flaherty greeted him with a single scoring Schoop and, after Kim walked, Machado drove in Flaherty with a single, making it 8-7 Baltimore.

Neither team scored in the fourth or fifth. Clay Buchholz took the mound for the Sox starting the fourth and pitched two scoreless innings in his second relief appearance. The Sox tied the game in the top of the fifth when Hanigan hit a grounder to short and Machado, after making a great stop, threw the ball away and Hanigan ended up on second. Pedroia drove him in with a single to right to make it 8-8.

In the last of the sixth, Buchholz walked Davis and Trumbo to start the inning and Wieters hit what looked like an easy double play ball to Pedroia which went though him for an error and Davis scored. Alvarez singled to left to load the bases and Flaherty drove in another with a ground ball out, making it 10-8. In the last of the seventh, Buchholz gave up a single to Kim and walked Davis again. He was relieved by Matt Barnes who gave up a walk to Trumbo, a single to center by Wieters, scoring two, and another single to center by Schoop, making it 13-8.

Chris Young led off the Sox eighth with a solo homer to cut the lead to 13-9, Orioles. That was the scoring for the game as the Orioles won. There were 29 hits, 14 by the O's and nine by the Sox, including five homers by the Sox in a losing cause. Kelly gave up seven runs on seven hits and three walks, throwing 59 pitches, only 32 of which were strikes in 2 1/3 innings. Buchholz got the loss, giving up four runs, three earned and four walks in 3

1/3 innings. He was victimized by Pedroia's error in the sixth, which should have been a double play and might have gotten him out of that inning with no runs.

After the game, Kelly was optioned to Pawtucket and Noe Ramirez was brought up to fill the roster spot. After coming back from the disabled list on May 21 and flirting with a no hitter while throwing 6 1/3 innings of one hit ball, Kelly had had two horrible outings in a row.

The Sox loss dropped them to two games up on second place Baltimore but, perhaps more importantly, the Blue Jays, who were coming into Boston for a three game series starting Friday, beat the Yankees 7-0, for their third straight win and moved to within four games of the Sox.

In the finale, at Baltimore, on Thursday night, Rick Porcello started for the Sox against Baltimore's Ubaldo Jimenez and it was scoreless until the last of the fourth when Machado singed and, with one out, Trumbo homered to make it 2-0 Baltimore. Jimenez had held the Sox hitless for four until Ramirez singled to begin the fifth but he got the next three batters in order.

In the last of the fifth, Flaherty singled and Jones homered to make it 4-0, O's. The Sox batted around in the sixth. After Vazquez doubled to start the inning, Betts walked and Pedroia singled to right to load the bases. Bogaerts singled to left driving in two and extending his consecutive game hitting streak to 26. Ortiz then hit his 16th homer, a three run shot to right, to put the Sox up 5-4.

Trumbo led off the sixth for the O's with another homer, his 17th of the year, to tie the score. In the seventh, with Ross on in relief of Porcello, Flaherty walked, Pena singled and, after two were out, Tazawa replaced Ross on the mound. Machado greeted him with a three run homer to make it 8-5. The Orioles added four in the eighth on solo homers by Alvarez and Jones, his second of the game, and a two run homer by rookie catcher Francisco Pena, son of former Red Sox Player and Coach Tony Pena to make it 12-5. The Orioles had hit homers in five consecutive innings and had seven for the game.

The Sox got two in the ninth on singles by Swihart, Young, Betts and Bogaerts but it was too little, too late as the Orioles won 12-7 and got back to within one game of the first place Sox. Porcello went six innings, giving up five runs on six hits but Ross got the loss.

They were going home for a three game series with the Toronto Blue Jays who had won eight of their last 10, including a three game sweep of the Yankees they completed with a 7-0 win the previous night and were now just 3 ½ games behind the Sox in third place.

R. A. Dickey started for Toronto in Game 1 against David Price. The Blue Jays got two in the first on a two run homer by Edward Encarnacion. The Sox came back with one in their half when Betts walked moved to third when Pedroia and Bogaerts each grounded out and scored on a passed ball to make it 2-1. In the Jays fourth, Devon Travis grounded to Shaw at third who threw the ball away allowing Travis to reach second. Pillar then singled to left to move Travis to third and he scored when Barney hit into a double play to make it 3-1.

In the top of the eighth, Uehara relieved Price and gave up a two run homer to Travis to make it 5-1. The Sox got another in the last of the eighth when Bogaerts walked, Ortiz hit his second double of the game and his 25th of the year and Ramirez grounded out to score Bogaerts. Reliever Joe Biagini then struck out Shaw and Roberto Osuna was brought in and got Bradley to pop out to end the eighth with the score 5-2.

Despite singles by Swihart and Pedroia in the ninth, Osuna held the Sox scoreless and the game ended 5-2, Toronto. Bogaerts came to the plate with two outs as the potential tying run and struck out ending the game and his 26 game hitting streak.

Dickey had had a no hitter going into the sixth inning when Ortiz led off with his first double of the game. He went 6 2/3 innings, giving up just one run on two hits. Price got his second loss, going seven innings and giving up three runs, two earned, on six hits.

The Orioles beat the Yankees 6-5 to move back into a tie for first with the Sox and Toronto moved to 3 ½ back.

Steven Wright started Game 2 against Toronto's Ace Marcus Stroman. The Sox scored first in the second when Shaw doubled to center and scored on Swihart's single to make it 1-0. In the Boston third, Pedroia walked, Bogaerts doubled and Ortiz singled to right to score them both and make it 3-0.

The Jays got one back in the fourth as Smoak singled to drive in Saunders. The Sox made it 4-1 in the last of the fourth when Bradley singled, stole second and scored on Betts' single to right. In the Toronto fifth, with runners on second and third and two out, Wright struck out Saunders but the ball got away from Hanigan and both runners scored, making it 4-3.

In the Boston fifth, Bogaerts singled to left and Ortiz grounded to third. Bogaerts went all the way to third on the throw to get Ortiz as Toronto left third uncovered. He then scored on Shaw's single to make it 5-3. Barnes relieved Wright in the sixth and walked Travis who then went to second on a wild pitch, stole third and scored on a ground out to make it 5-4. The Sox added a run in the sixth when Swihart walked and scored when Betts doubled to left and it was 6-4.

Barnes got through the seventh without a score and Tazawa and Kimbrel held the Jays in the eighth and ninth. Wright got the win to make his record 6-4 and Kimbrel got his 13th save. Both Swihart, who jammed his left ankle when trying to catch a foul ball off the side wall in left field, and Hanigan, who had a recurrence of a neck strain, had to be removed from the game. Both players were placed on the 15 day disabled list, leaving the Sox without a back up catcher.

They brought up Rusney Castillo and Heath Hembree to fill the roster slots and optioned Noe Ramirez to Pawtucket to make room for catcher Sandy Leon whose contract they purchased from Pawtucket to give them a back up catcher for Christian Vazquez.

The win put the Sox back in first alone, one game up on the Orioles who lost to the Yankees, 8-6, and 3 ½ up on third place Toronto.

In the final game with Toronto, Eduardo Rodriguez started for the Sox against Marco Estrada. Joey Bautista led off the game with a homer to left center to make it 1-0 Toronto. In the Jays third, Barney hit a solo homer to left and, after Donaldson walked, Encarnacion hit a homer to left to make it 4-0. The Jays added another in the sixth when Martin homered with no one on base.

In the meantime, Estrada was holding the Red Sox hitless going into the eighth. He got Jackie Bradley to pop out to start the eighth but Chris Young then homered to break up the no hitter and make it 5-1. Estrada got out of the inning and it was 5-1 going to the ninth.

Pedroia led off the Boston ninth with a double to left and Closer Osuna replaced Estrada. After one out, Ortiz hit his 26th double of the season to score Pedroia. Castillo then ran for Ortiz. After Osuna struck out Shaw for the second out, Ramirez doubled to center to score Castillo and it was 5-3. Bradley then hit a soft line drive single to right to score Ramirez and it was 5-4 with the tying run on base. Young singled to left to put the tying run in scoring position at second. Hernandez then batted for Vazquez and struck out and the rally had fallen one run short.

Rodriguez, who went 5 2/3 innings, giving up all five runs, four of them earned and all on homers got the loss and Estrada who gave up just two hits and two runs in eight innings got the win.

Baltimore beat the Yankees 3-1 to move back into a virtual tie with the Sox for first with Toronto in third 2 ½ games back. Despite losing six of ten against the Division, the Sox were fortunate to still be tied for first.

The following column appeared in the Biddeford Journal Tribune, in Biddeford, Maine, on June 5, 2016.

WHO IS STEVEN WRIGHT?

What makes a pitcher, who has spent nine seasons in the Minor Leagues with a 3.79 earned run average into a Major League pitcher with a 5-4 record and an ERA of 2.45, the best on the team with the best record in the American League? Apparently, at least in the case of Steven Wright, of the Red Sox, the answer is, a knuckle ball.

Wright, who was born in Torrance, California, on August 30, 1984, was drafted by the Cleveland Indians in the second round of the 2006 Amateur Draft. He had been drafted by the San Diego Padres in the 26th round of the 2003 draft but did not sign. He opted to play ball at the University of Hawaii, where he was named a second team All American in his Junior Year.

He signed with the Indians on July 3, 2006 and began his long trip to the Major Leagues in A Ball that year, winning seven and losing nine, with a 5.67 ERA in 27 starts. He progressed through the Indians system, having his best year, mainly as a reliever with just six starts, at AA Akron where he won 10 and lost none and had a 2.48 ERA in 2009.

In 2011, while being shuffled between the Lake County Captains in the Class A Midwest League, The Kinston Indians in the Carolina League, the Akron Aeros in the AA Eastern League and the Columbus Clippers in the AAA International League, he developed a knuckle ball. That year, he was 4-8 with a 4.58 ERA.

On July 31, 2012, he was traded by the Indians to the Red Sox for first baseman Lars Anderson. Anderson, a first baseman/outfielder, who had played briefly with the Sox has never played in the Big Leagues again and is now playing for the Los Angeles Dodgers AAA affiliate Oklahoma City.

In 2012, Wright was 10-7 between Akron, the Cleveland affiliate, where he was 9-6 before being traded and 1-1 between Portland and Pawtucket with the Sox system.

In 2013, the Red Sox called him up on April 16 to replace Joel Hanrahan, who had suffered a right hamstring strain and he made his debut on April 23 in relief of Alfredo Aceves against the Oakland Athletics, going 3 2/3 innings and giving up five runs on six hits in a game the Sox lost 13-0, being shut out by Bartolo Colon, now the ageless Mets wonder.

He won two and lost none that year with a 5.40 ERA while shuttling back and forth from Boston to Pawtucket, where he was 8-7 with a 2.49 ERA in 20 starts. In 2014, he was 5-5 at Pawtucket with a 3.41 ERA and threw just 21 innings for the Sox. He missed the last six weeks of the 2014 season after being bit on the head by a fly ball while running in the outfield before a game with the Sox.

Last year, he won five and lost four with a 4.09 ERA in nine starts and seven relief appearances, throwing just 72 2/3 innings. He also started eight games at Pawtucket, winning two and losing five and posting a 3.81 ERA.

Since developing the knuckleball in 2011, he has won 26 and lost 24 in the minors and won 12 and lost nine in the Majors.

Wright was expected to work out of the Red Sox bullpen this year but, when Eduardo Rodriguez suffered that freak injury to his knee, he was pressed into service as a starter. Through Friday, he had started 10 games for the Sox and had won five while losing four with a 2.45 ERA.

He had thrown three complete games, tied for the most in the American League, and had thrown six or more innings in each of his starts except one. In that start, against Houston on May 13, he gave up five runs in 4 1/3 innings but did not get a decision. He has only given up as many as three runs in any other start once. In the four games that he had lost he had given up just eight earned runs, in 26 2/3 innings, for a 2.70 ERA and, in the five that he had won, he had given up only six runs, in 38 2/3 innings, for a 1.41 ERA.

In his last five starts, he has thrown three complete games including a complete game win in the opener of last week's crucial four game series against the powerful Baltimore Orioles. In that game, he gave up just four hits, three of them in the fifth inning when the Orioles got their only two runs, and held them hitless from the fifth on. He threw a career high 122 pitches in that game, 75 of them for strikes, while walking five and striking out seven.

For a player who, two years ago, was considering quitting baseball, the knuckle ball has been like magic. Unlike most knuckle ball pitchers whose offerings have more vertical movement than horizontal, Wright's knucklers seem to have more side to side movement, causing his regular catcher, Ryan Hanigan, many frustrating moments trying to capture them.

As Willie Stargell once said 'Throwing a knuckleball for a strike is like throwing a butterfly with hiccups across the street into your neighbor's mailbox.' Steven Wright appears to have mastered the art of throwing that knuckleball at just the right time for the Red Sox.

CARL H. JOHNSON
June 5, 2016

CHAPTER 11

OFF TO THE WEST

JUNE 6-16

The Sox had Monday off and flew to San Francisco for a two game set, Tuesday and Wednesday, with the Giants. The Giants, with a record of 35-24 were in first place in the Western Division of the National League, four games ahead of the second place Dodgers.

Rick Porcello started for the Sox against Albert Suarez for the Giants. The Sox got one in the second on doubles by Bradley and Young and added another in the third when Betts doubled to left, went to third when Pedroia grounded out and scored on a single to deep short by Bogaerts. Jarrett Parker led off the Giants third with a solo homer to make it 2-1.

The Giants went up 3-2 in the fourth on singles by Joe Panik, Matt Duffy and Brandon Belt which loaded the bases. Brandon Crawford then walked to force in Panik and Duffy scored when Blanco hit into a double play. In the Sox seventh, Bradley walked, stole second and went to third on a throwing error by the catcher and then scored when Ortiz, batting for Vazquez, grounded out, to tie the score at 3-3.

Ross relieved Porcello in the seventh and he, Uehara and Tazawa held the Giants scoreless through the ninth. In the Boston tenth, with Santiago Casilla on the mound for the Giants, Sandy Leon led off with a double in his first appearance of the year since being recalled from Pawtucket. Hernandez, hitting for Tazawa, drew a walk. Betts then reached on a bunt single to load the bases. Pedroia grounded to third and Leon was forced out at the plate. Bogaerts then hit a line drive single to center to score Hernandez and Betts to make it 5-3.

Kimbrel, despite giving up a lead off single, got the Giants in the tenth for his 14th save. Tazawa, who had pitched a scoreless ninth, got his first win of the year. Baltimore beat the Royals for the second night in a row to stay one half game up on Boston and Toronto lost to Detroit to fall 4 ½ games back.

Game 2 of the two game series on Wednesday night would feature Boston Ace David Price against the Giants' Ace Madison Bumgarner. As expected, the game was a pitchers' duel with both starters giving up just one run though the sixth inning. The Sox got theirs on a homer to left by Young in the fourth and the Giants got it back on a homer by first baseman Brandon Belt in their half of the fourth.

Bumgarner was removed after sixth, having thrown 101 pitches. Price gave up a lead off, first pitch homer by Mac Williamson to lead off the eighth and that was the scoring. The Giants used five relievers to hold the Sox scoreless the rest of the way and win, 2-1. Price went the route for Boston, giving up just one more hit and striking out seven for his third loss. The Sox could manage just five hits against Giants' pitching and dropped to 1 ½ games behind Baltimore who beat Kansas City 4-0.

The Sox now traveled to Minnesota for a three game set with the Twins, starting Friday night. The Twins were in last place in the Central Division with a record of 18-40, the second worst record in all of baseball behind the Atlanta Braves. The Orioles won on Thursday night, while the Sox were off, to extend their lead over second place Boston to two games.

Steven Wright started Game 1 against the Twins and held them scoreless through seven. A throwing error by Hanley Ramirez on a grounder by Eduardo Nunez, who went to third on a passed ball and scored on a ground out, gave the Twins their first and only run of the game in the eighth. Meantime, after being held scoreless by the Twins' Tyler Duffey for four innings, the Sox erupted for three in the fifth on singles by Vazquez and Pedroia and a three run homer by Bogaerts.

They got three more in the sixth on Bradley's double to right, high off the wall, a single by Shaw and another by Vazquez driving in Bradley. Pedroia added his second double of the game to drive in Vazquez. Bogaerts then got his fourth hit of the game, a single, driving in Pedroia to make it 6-0.

The Sox added two in the ninth on singles by Ortiz and Ramirez and Bradley's fifth triple of the year to make the final 8-1. Wright gave up seven hits and just the one unearned run to earn his 7th victory against four losses and lower his ERA to a league leading 2.09. Bogaerts' four hits raised his league leading average to .349 and Pedroia's first inning double extended his hitting streak to 16 games. Bogaerts led all of baseball with 88 hits and, amazingly Pedroia and Betts, with 77 and 76 respectively, were fourth and fifth in all of baseball.

Boston moved to one game behind the Orioles who lost to Toronto, 4-3, and Toronto was now 4 ½ back in third place.

The Sox got off to a fast start in Game 2 at Minnesota, scoring four in the first. Betts beat out an infield single on a grounder past the mound and Bogaerts drove him in with a double to left. After Ramirez walked, Bradley homered deep to right to make it 4-0. Eduardo Rodriguez started for the Sox and got through the first three innings scoreless despite giving up three walks. In the fourth, he walked Dozier, Kepler singled and Suzuki homered to make it 4-3. He gave up another in the fourth when Mauer singled, went to second on a passed ball and third on Dozier's single. Plouffe hit a sac fly to center to score him with the tying run.

The Sox went back ahead in the sixth when Bogaerts singled to left and, when Ortiz grounded to second, beat the attempted force at second and kept right on running to reach third which was unprotected because of the shift. He then scored on a sac fly by Bradley to make it 5-4.

The Sox bats came back to life in the eighth and ninth as they sent 19 batters to the plate, scoring five runs in each inning to make it 15-4. Bogaerts had a two run homer and Betts, Young and Leon all had two run scoring singles in the two innings.

Rodriguez was removed after 4 2/3 innings, with the score tied 4-4 and relievers Hembree, Ross, Tazawa, Uehara and Buchholz held the Twins to one hit the rest of the way to make the final 15-4. Hembree got the win improving his record to 3-0.

The Sox had 15 hits, including four each by Bogaerts and Leon but Pedroia was hitless, snapping his streak at 16 games. Bogaerts second four hit game in a row raised his Major League leading average to .358. Leon, with four hits and a walk in five at bats had now gone 5-5 since being brought in from Pawtucket as backup catcher. Ortiz, with a 3-5 day, raised his average to .346, second to Bogaerts in the American League.

Baltimore lost to Toronto 11-6 to move the Sox into a tie for first with the O's again with the teams having identical 36-25 records.

The Twins got off to a quick lead in the first of Game 3 against Porcello when Nunez led off with a single, stole second, went to third on a ground out and scored when Mauer grounded to third. They added one in the second on a single to center by Escobar and, when Bogaerts booted a grounder up the middle which should have been a double play, Escobar went to third and scored when Buxton grounded into a force at second, making it 2-0.

Former Boston College star Pat Dean, who started for the Twins, held the Sox scoreless through four and Chris Young homered in the fifth to make it 2-1. With two outs and runners on first and second in the Twins sixth, Bogaerts made his second error of the game, a throwing error on a routine ground ball, and one runner scored to make it 3-1, Minnesota. Escobar then singled to center to drive in one more and make it 4-1.

In the Sox eighth, Hernandez, hitting for Vazquez, walked to lead off the inning and Betts and Pedroia singled to load the bases. Bogaerts then hit a shot into the hole between third and short. Nunez made a great stop and threw wildly to second missing the force and allowing Martinez and Betts to score. With Bogaerts on first, Ortiz hit into his second double play of the game but Pedroia scored the tying run to make it 4-4. Ramirez then walked, stole second and went to third on the wild throw to second. Bradley then struck out to end the rally.

Uehara and Tazawa held the Twins scoreless in the eighth and ninth and the game went into the tenth still tied 4-4. In the top of the ninth, with two outs, Bogaerts beat out an infield hit with a head first slide into first, then stole second, but Ortiz struck out to end the threat.

In the bottom of the tenth, Matt Barnes in relief of Tazawa, walked Mauer to lead off the inning and the cleanup hitter,

Plouffe, sacrificed him to second. Dozier then singled to center with Mauer stopping at third. With the winning run on third and one out, Farrell pulled Betts into the infield from right field to go with five infielders to try to cut down the run at the plate. Max Kepler then beat that strategy with a long walk off homer to center to win the game for the Twins 7-4.

Porcello, although giving up just one earned run in seven innings got no decision again and Barnes got the loss. The Sox could manage only one earned run on seven hits after scoring 15 the day before. They had Monday off and were scheduled to start a three game series at home against Baltimore on Tuesday. The Orioles had lost to the Jays again to keep them tied with the Sox in first but the Jays were now just 2 ½ back in third.

Game 1 featured Oriole Ace Chris Tillman,8-1, against Red Sox Ace, David Price, 7-3, in Fenway. Price got off to a rocky start, giving up a single to Joey Rickard and a homer just inside the foul pole by Manny Machado with one out in the first to put the O's up 2-0. Price proceeded to set down the next 19 batters in order before giving up a single to Mark Trumbo in the seventh. He got out of the inning with no further scoring and Jackie Bradley made it 2-1 with a blast over the center field wall in the last of the seventh.

The Sox had had opportunities but failed to capitalize against Tillman. In the second, Ortiz doubled to lead off the inning and Ramirez walked. Tillman then struck out Bradley and Young before walking Shaw to load the bases. Vazquez then hit into a force out and the inning was over. Pedroia doubled with one out in the third but was left stranded when Bogaerts grounded out, moving him to third and Ortiz struck out.

Jonathan Schoop led off the eighth with a homer for Baltimore and it was 3-1. In the last of the eighth, with Givens on in relief for the O's, Betts doubled to lead off and, after Pedroia flied out to right, Bogaerts walked. Baltimore Closer Zach Britton came in to pitch and Ortiz struck out for the second time with runners in scoring position, Ramirez singled to score Betts and make it 3-2 but Britton got Bradley to tap back to the mound to end the rally.

The Sox brought in Closer Kimbrel in the ninth and he got the O's in order with two strike outs. Britton struck out Young, Shaw and Castillo, hitting for Vazquez, in the ninth for his 20th save. Price got the loss making him 7-4 and Tillman got his ninth win. Price went eight innings, giving up the three runs on five hits while striking out 11 and Tillman went seven innings, giving up just one run on five hits. The Sox were able to manage only seven hits as they fell one game behind the O's.

In Game 2, Wright started for Boston and Gausman for Baltimore. The Sox got on the board first in the last of the second when Ramirez walked and, after two were out, Young singled him to third and Shaw doubled to left to score Ramirez and make it 1-0. In the third, singles by Betts and Pedroia put men on first and third. Bogaerts singled to deep short to score Betts and Ortiz singled to right to score Pedroia. Ramirez then hit his fifth home run, his first in over a month, over the Green Monster, to make it 6-0 Boston.

Wright held the O's scoreless until the seventh when Rickard singled and Jones hit a homer to left to make it 6-2. In the eighth, with one out, Wright walked Davis and Tazawa came on in relief of Wright. After getting a fly out for the second out, Tazawa gave up a double to right to Wieters, scoring Davis, and Schoop singled to right, scoring Wieters and making it 6-4. Tazawa then got out of the inning.

In the top of the ninth, with the score still 6-4, Kimbrel came in and set down the O's in order for his 15th save. Wright, who went 7 1/3 innings, giving up three runs on six hits, got his eighth victory against four losses. The first five hitters in the Sox order, Betts, Pedroia, Bogaerts, Ortiz and Ramirez all got three hits in the 13 hit attack. The win put the Sox back into a tie for first with Baltimore and the Blue Jays, who beat the Phillies 7-2, moved to two games back, in third.
While this was going on, Ichiro Suzuki got his 4,257th hit in professional baseball in San Diego with a double for Miami in the ninth inning of the Marlins loss. Suzuki, who had 1,278 hits in

Japan before coming to the Seattle Mariners at age 27, now has 2,979 in MLB, just 21 shy of the 3,000 hit mark.

In Game 3, the Red Sox ran into a surprising buzz saw on the mound for the Orioles. Tyler Wilson, the O's right hander, who they had defeated on May 30, scoring three runs on eight hits in 6 2/3 innings against him, held them to one hit for six innings and three hits for eight innings while shutting them out. While Wilson, who entered the game with a 2-5 record and a 4.73 ERA was completely stifling the Boston offense, the O's got a two run homer from Adam Jones in the third, his second in two days, to make it 2-0.

They got another in the fourth on a double by Jones scoring Paul Janish who had singled and added two in the fifth when Machado doubled to start the inning and, when Chris Davis singled to score him, John Farrell pulled starter Eduardo Rodriguez after another disappointing outing.

Barnes came on in relief and struck out Matt Wieters but then gave up a run scoring double to Jonathan Schoop before getting out of the inning. That made it 5-0 and it stayed that way until Ortiz hit his 520th homer off reliever Brad Brach with two out in the ninth to make the final score 5-1.

Rodriguez, who gave up five runs on eight hits, lost his second game and saw his ERA go up to 6.97. It was his third consecutive poor start in June and he had now given up 14 earned runs in just 14 2/3 innings in the month. The only bright spot for the Sox was the fact that Clay Buchholz, coming in to pitch the last three innings, held the O's scoreless on two hits while striking out four and, more importantly, not walking anyone.

The Sox fell into second place, again, one game behind Baltimore and just one game ahead of third place Toronto who beat up on the Phillies 13-2. The Seattle Mariners, in second place in the Western Division of the American League were next in to Boston starting a three game series on Friday night, June 17.

CHAPTER 12

THE WHEELS COME OFF

JUNE 17-26

They now faced a ten game stretch where they played Central and Western Division teams. Seattle was coming to Fenway for a three game series, followed by the Chicago White Sox for four. The Sox would then go to Texas for a three game series with the first place Rangers.

Roenis Elias, the 28 year old left hander, acquired from Seattle, was brought up from Pawtucket to start Game 1 against his former team. At Seattle, he had been 15-20 in 2014 and 2015 and was 4-3 at Pawtucket this year with a 3.54 ERA. He had made one appearance with the Sox, in relief, on April 23, at Houston, where he gave up three runs on four hits and two walks in 1 2/3 innings.

Ketel Marte hit his first pitch high off the wall in left for a single and Franklin Gutierrez took one ball before depositing the third pitch of the game in the center field seats to make it 2-0. Gutierrez led off the third, hitting the first pitch over the left field wall for his second homer on three pitches and it was 3-0. In the fourth inning, the Mariners loaded the bases with two outs and Gutierrez, on the third pitch of the at bat, hit a double to the base of the wall in right field to clear the bases and make it 6-0 with all six runs driven in by Gutierrez. Robinson Cano then singled to left to score Gutierrez with the seventh run but was thrown out by Chris Young trying to stretch it to a double to end the inning, 7-0.

The Sox got two in the last of the fourth on a single by Bogaerts and a home run to straight away center by Ortiz. It was his 18th of the year and the 521st of his career. Heath Hembree replaced Elias, who had given up seven runs on seven hits and three walks, to start the fifth and held the Mariners scoreless until Cano led off the seventh with a solo homer to make it 8-2. In the bottom of the seventh, a single by Shaw and a double by Leon, followed by two sac flies by Betts and Pedroia made it 8-4. Tommy Layne shut out the Mariners in order in the eighth and ninth.

In the Sox ninth, despite singles by Young and Leon, the Sox didn't score and the final was 8-4. Leon's single was his ninth hit in 13 at bats, his third hit of the game, since being brought up when Hanigan and Swihart were injured. It was his third three hit game in that stretch and his average was an amazing .692.

Baltimore was beaten by Toronto, 13-3, so the Sox remained one game back but the Blue Jays had moved into a virtual tie for second with the Sox, only four percentage points behind.

In Game 2, Porcello started for the Sox and gave up a run in the first when singles by Martin, Smith and Cano loaded the bases and, when Cruz hit into a 6-4-3 double play, Martin scored. In the second, Adam Lind hit a solo homer on a 3-2 pitch to make it 2-0.

That was all the scoring for Seattle as Porcello shut them out through the sixth and Tazawa, Uehara and Kimbrel closed them down in the seventh, eighth and ninth with only one baserunner, a single off Tazawa in the seventh.

In the meantime, the Sox got one on a solo homer by Bradley with two outs in the fourth. In the fifth, after Young and Vazquez singled, Betts drove in Young with another single to tie the game and Vazquez scored when Pedroia hit into a double play. Bogaerts then homered to left to make it 5-2. The Sox added a final run in the eighth when Ramirez doubled and Bradley lined out to Cano at second. When Cano tried to double Ramirez off second, his throw was mishandled by the shortstop and Ramirez scored to make the final 6-2.

While the Red Sox were winning, Baltimore beat Toronto, 4-2, and maintained their one game lead against the Red Sox and moved to two up on third place Toronto.

Boston sent David Price to the mound to try to take the rubber game of the three game series from Seattle. Price gave up a solo homer to Franklin Guttierez to lead off the fourth and make it 1-0. The Sox tied it in the sixth when Bogaerts led off with a single to left and Ortiz singled to center, sending Bogaerts to third. Ramirez then hit a grounder to short, forcing Ortiz but scoring Bogaerts. Mookie Betts led off the seventh with a homer to left center and the Sox were up 2-1.

That was all the scoring as Price went eight innings, giving up just the one run on eight hits while striking out seven and walking no one for his eighth win with four losses. Kimbrel pitched the ninth, striking out the side in order to earn his 16th save.

Baltimore beat Toronto 11-6 so the Red Sox remained one game back while Toronto fell to three back, in third place. The Chicago White Sox were coming in to Fenway on Monday for a four game series. The White Sox were in fourth place in the Central Division, three games below .500 and 5 ½ games behind division leading Cleveland.

David Wright pitched another great game against the White Sox in Game 1, going nine innings and giving up just one unearned run on five hits. The Chicago run came in the second when Brett Lawrie doubled to left, went to third on a fly out and scored on a passed ball. The Sox tied it in the eighth on a single to left by Young, a walk to Shaw and a single by Vazquez, scoring Young.

The game was tied at 1-1 after nine and Kimbrel came in to relieve Wright. He walked the first batter, Avisail Garcia on four pitches and gave up a single to left to J. B. Schutt. He struck out the next batter and Adam Eaton hit into a force play at second to make it two outs and runners on first and third. Jose Abreau then doubled to score two and it was 3-1 Chicago.

In the last of the tenth, David Robertson held the Red Sox scoreless and the ChiSox had won the first game. Kimbrel got the loss, his third without a win. The Sox fell to 39-30 but stayed one game down on Baltimore who lost to Texas, 4-3.

After five games out of the bullpen, Buchholz started Game 2 against Chicago. Anderson led off for the White Sox and hit Buchholz's first pitch of the game for a homer and Eaton hit a double to center on the second pitch. When Abreau grounded to short, Eaton moved to third, and then scored on a sac fly by Cabrera to make it 2-0.

The Sox got one back in the third when Shaw and Leon singled and, when Deven Marrero lined out to center, Shaw took third and scored on a sac fly to left by Betts to make it 2-1. Pedroia then singled and Bogaerts walked but Chris Sale struck out Ramirez to end the inning with the Sox down. Todd Frazier homered off Buchholz in the fourth to make it 3-1 and that was the scoring for the game as the Red Sox lost their second in a row by the same score.

Sale, who started for Chicago, went seven innings, giving up just one run on four hits. Buchholz lasted five, only giving up four hits but the two homers were the difference. Barnes and Layne combined to shut out the White Sox the rest of the way. Buchholz got his seventh loss with only three wins and Sale went to 12-2. Robertson got his eighteenth save for Chicago.

The Orioles lost to the San Diego Padres, 17-10, so the Red Sox stayed one game back in second place.

Chicago scored first in the second inning of Game 3. Eaton walked and Cabrera drove him in with a double to center. They made it 2-0 in the third when Coates doubled, moved to third on a ground out and scored when Shaw mishandled Abreau's grounder at third.

Leon walked and Betts and Pedroia singled to load the bases in the Boston third. Bogaerts singled to center to drive in two and Ortiz singled to right to score Pedroia. Bradley then reached on a grounder and Bogaerts scored to make it 4-2. Chicago came back to tie it in the sixth on a single by Cabrera and a homer by Frazier, his 21st.

In the Boston sixth, Ramirez homered to right center, his sixth. Leon walked and Pedroia singled to center, sending Leon to third. Leon then scored on a sac fly by Betts and it was 6-4, Boston.

In the Chicago eighth, with Uehara pitching for Boston, Eaton singled and Cabrera homered. Lawrie then hit a solo homer and it was 7-6, Chicago. Chicago added another on an RBI single by Cabrera, making the final 8-6. Uehara got the loss and the blown save.

Baltimore beat San Diego, 7-2, to move to two games ahead of Boston and Toronto was in third, just one half game behind the Red Sox.

Rick Porcello started for the Sox trying to salvage one game of the four game set in an unusual afternoon game on a Thursday designed to give the Sox time to travel to Texas for the start of a three game set there.

Chicago got two in the first when singles by Anderson, Eaton and Abreau, loaded the bases. Anderson scored when Cabrera hit into a double play and Eaton scored on a wild pitch. Singles by Lawrie, Avila and Shuck scored another in the fourth and it was 3-0.

Chris Young strained a right ham string after being walked in the second and was replaced by Ryan LaMarre in left. Boston came back in the fifth when Pedroia doubled in Betts who had singled to make it 3-1. Cabrera tripled and scored on Frazier's sac fly in the sixth to make it 4-1. Ortiz and LaMarre, walked and Bradley was hit by a pitch to load the bases for the Red Sox in the sixth. Ramirez then got an infield hit with two runs scoring on a throwing error. Leon, pinch hitting for Vazquez, then singled to drive in a run and Ramirez scored on a fielder's choice to make it 5-4 Boston.

In the Chicago seventh Anderson and Eaton singled and Abreau hit his 11th homer to make it 7-5, Chicago. The Sox got one in the seventh after Pedroia walked, Bogaerts singled and Ortiz was intentionally walked to load the bases. Shaw, hitting for LaMarre, then hit a sac fly to right and it was 7-6. Hernandez doubled and scored on Pedroia's single to tie the game at 7-7. Shaw stayed in the game and played left field for the first time in his Major League career.

In the tenth, Kimbrel who had come on and pitched a perfect ninth loaded the bases with no outs and got out of it with a pop out and two strikeouts. In the Sox tenth, Hernandez walked, Betts hit into a force play, Pedroia walked and Bogaerts singled to center to drive in the winning run on a walk off as Boston won 8-7.

Kimbrel got the win, his first against three losses. Porcello had lasted just 5 1/3, giving up four runs on eight hits. Sandy Leon continued his hot hitting with his average at .524 since being brought back up.

The Sox win moved them to 1 ½ games behind idle Baltimore and avoided the sweep. They now headed for Texas and a three game series with the Rangers who were in first place in the west, 10 games ahead with a 47-26 record. The Rangers had won eight of their last 10.

David Price started for the Sox in Game 1 and Shin-Soo Choo met him with a lead off homer in the first. Then singles by Ian Desmond, Adrian Beltre and Ryan Rua loaded the bases with no outs. Prince Fielder then grounded to Ramirez at first and he started a rare 3-2-3 double play, forcing Desmond at the plate and getting Fielder at first. Elvis Andrus then singled to left scoring Beltre and Rua and it was 3-0 before the Red Sox came to bat.

Desmond singled to drive in Bobby Wilson, who had doubled, in the second. The Rangers got two more on four singles in the third and Barnes replaced Price with the score 6-0. Barnes got out of the inning with no further scoring.

In the Sox fourth, Ortiz singled and Ramirez hit his seventh homer to center to get the Sox on the board at 6-2. The Rangers came back with a homer by Fielder in the last of the fourth to make it 7-2. In the sixth, Ramirez walked and Bradley homered to make it 7-4. Layne and Hembree held the Rangers scoreless in the sixth, seventh and eighth and it went to the ninth 7-4.

With two outs and Bradley on first by way of a walk, Leon hit for Vazquez and for the second night in a row, delivered with a double, scoring Bradley. Betts then homered to left center to tie the game at 7-7. Pedroia walked and Bogaerts singled him to third. Pedroia raced home with the winning run on a wild pitch to put the Sox up 8-7.

In the last of the ninth, Uehara struck out the 5, 6 and 7 hitters in the Rangers order to earn the save as the Sox completed an unlikely comeback and won their second game in a row by an 8-7 score.

Hembree got his fourth win and Uehara his second save.

In Game 2, with Wright on the mound for the Sox, Boston scored first on a solo homer by Ramirez, his eighth, to right center in the second. The Rangers got three in the fourth. Desmond hit a lead off homer, Beltre walked, Odor reached on a bunt and Andrus walked to load the bases. Morehead then singled to right scoring two to make it 3-1.

In the Sox fifth Bradley and Brentz singled and Vazquez walked to load the bases. Betts then singled in Bradley to make it 3-2. Wright was a victim of his own defense in the last of the fifth as errors by Bogaerts and Ramirez, a run scoring single by Beltre, a three run triple by Andrus and a run scoring wild pitch by Robbie Ross in relief of Wright, gave the Rangers five unearned runs and an 8-2 lead.

In the Sox sixth, Bradley doubled in Bogaerts and Ortiz, who had walked, making it 8-3. The Rangers added two more in the seventh making the final 10-3.

Wright got the loss, his fifth with eight wins, giving up eight runs, only three earned, on seven hits and throwing 98 pitches in just 4 2/3 innings. The Sox fell to three games behind Baltimore who beat Tampa Bay 8-6. They were at 41-33, just eight games over .500 and had lost six of their last ten while Baltimore was winning seven of ten.

Clay Buchholz was back as the Red Sox starter in Game 3 after having lost to the White Sox just five days earlier. He quickly gave up three runs in the last of the first on five singles, falling behind 3-0. The Sox did not get on the board until the sixth when Bryce Brentz hit a solo homer to left to make it 3-1. In the last of the sixth, Beltre reached on a rare error by Bogaerts at short and Prince Fielder hit the next pitch for a homer and it was 5-1. Texas added another in the seventh on a Beltre RBI single to make it 6-1.

The Sox got their final run in the eighth when Ortiz drove in Bogaerts with a single to right to make the final 6-2. Buchholz got his eighth loss with just three wins and raised his ERA to 5.90.

The Sox had lost six of the ten games against the Central and Western Division teams. Baltimore was beating Tampa Bay 12-5 while this was going on and moved four games ahead of the Sox.

CHAPTER 13

TO THE ALL STAR BREAK

JUNE 27-JULY 10

The Sox left for a three game series with the Tampa Bay Rays at Tropicana Field beginning Monday. The Rays had lost 11 in a row and were wallowing in last place in the East.

The Rays wasted no time in getting off to a good start against Eduardo Rodriguez, who started for the Sox. They got five in the last of the first on four singles and two doubles and added four in the third including homers by Jennings and Forsythe to go up 9-0. Rodriguez lasted just 2 2/3 innings, giving up nine runs on 11 hits.

The Sox could manage 12 hits and seven runs but the final was 13-7 as the Rays ended their losing streak with authority against an ineffective Red Sox pitching staff. Uehara, in relief in the eighth, walked the first batter and gave up a homer to Franklin and Kimbrel, pitching the last of the eighth, gave up a run on three singles.

The loss dropped the Sox to 41-35, just six games over .500 and left them 4 ½ games behind idle Baltimore and just one game ahead of third place Toronto.

Rick Porcello started Game 2 against the Rays at the Trop and went six innings, giving up just one run on five hits while striking out eight. The Sox got one in the second when Shaw led off with a homer, his eighth of the season. They got another on doubles by Betts and Ortiz in the third to go up 2-0. In the Rays fourth, Porcello loaded the bases on two walks and a single and forced in a run by walking Franklin to make it 2-1 with the bases loaded and no outs. He got out of it with no further damage, striking out two.

Bradley got the run back with an RBI double in the fifth and the

Sox were up 3-1. Singles by Pedroia, Bogaerts and Ramirez and a two run double by Shaw put them up 6-1 in the top of the seventh. Tazawa relieved Porcello in the seventh and gave up a solo homer to Miller.

The Sox added two in the ninth on two walks and a two run single by Shaw giving him five RBI's on the night and making the final 8-2. Porcello got the win, his ninth with only two losses and lowered his ERA to 3.78.

The Sox could do nothing with Matt Moore and two Rays relievers as they were shut out on five hits in Game 3. Brandon Guyer homered off Price to start the second and make it 1-0. In the Rays third, Forsythe and Miller singled and Longoria hit an RBI double. Jennings grounded back to Price and, when the Sox went for two unsuccessfully, Miller scored. Guyer then doubled to left to make it 4-0 and that was the scoring.

Price got his fifth loss, going 6 1/3, giving up all four runs on nine hits while striking out ten. Matt Moore held the Sox to three hits in seven innings.

The Sox fell to 42-36, just six games over .500 and 5 ½ games behind the Orioles in a tie for second with the Jays and had now lost seven of their last ten games. They had the next day, June 30, off and would face the L. A. Angels at home for a three game set starting July 1.

Steven Wright started for the Sox and held the Angels scoreless through five. The Sox got on the board early when Betts led off the first with a double, went to third on a ground out and scored on Bogaerts grounder to second. They got another in the fourth on back to back doubles by Shaw and Holt to make it 2-0. They added three in the fifth when Ortiz hit a solo homer, Bradley singled, Holt doubled him in and Vazquez scored Holt with a single and it was 5-0.

The Angels got four in the sixth on a double by Pujols, a hit batter, a walk and a grand slam by C. J. Cron, chasing Wright, who left ahead 5-4. At the start of the sixth, it was raining hard and Wright was obviously having trouble controlling his knuckler. Farrell appeared to be on the verge of removing him before the grand slam but held off one pitch too long.

Barnes, Tazawa and Uehara shut out the Angels through the eighth and Kimbrel, despite giving up a walk and a double in the ninth, held them at 5-4 for his 17th save.

Wright got the win and was now 9-5 with a 2.42 ERA. Baltimore lost to Seattle 5-2 so the Sox moved back to four games behind the O's in second place.

The Sox started 3-8 Clay Buchholz against the Angels in Game 2. He lasted just 4 1/3 innings, giving up seven runs, only three of them earned, and left behind 7-0. Hembree relieved him in the fifth and, before the inning was over, it was 9-0, California. The Sox got one back in the fifth when Betts doubled and scored on an error.

In the top of the seventh, California sent a total of 14 batters to the plate and scored 11 runs on nine hits, including home runs by Cron and Perez against relievers Robbie Ross and Pat Light to make it 20-1. Betts had a solo homer in the seventh and the Angels added a run in the eighth to make the final 21-2.

Buchholz got his ninth loss as the Angels got a total of 22 hits and were aided by four Red Sox errors. Fortunately, Baltimore lost to Seattle 12-6 so the Sox remained four games back.

In Game 3, the Red Sox started 28 year old Sean O'Sullivan, brought up from Pawtucket against the Angels. In the last of the fifth, the Sox got seven runs on six hits, including doubles by Ortiz, Ramirez and Leon, two singles and two walks, to go up 7-0.

Sullivan shut out California for five innings before giving up singles to Simmons and Escobar to start the sixth. Matt Barnes relieved him and gave up a double to Calhoun, scoring one. Trout then drove in another with a fielder's choice ground out and Pujols doubled to make it 7-3 before the inning was over. In the top of the seventh, with Tazawa on the mound for the Sox, the Angels got two more on a single by Petit and doubles by Simmons and Escobar to make it 7-5.

The Sox came back with three in their half of the seventh on singles by Bradley, Holt and Leon, a walk to Hernandez and another single by Pedroia to make it 10-5. Uehara and Layne shut down the Angels the rest of the way and the Sox won. O'Sullivan got the win, his second, giving up just two runs on three hits. Leon went 2-4 with three RBI's to raise his batting average to .457.

Baltimore lost to Seattle, 9-4, so the Sox gained a game to move to three behind the O's with the Jays just ½ game back in third.

The Rangers came into Boston for a series beginning on July 4. Rick Porcello started for the Sox and gave up four runs on five singles before getting out of the first inning. The Sox got one back in the last of the first on a bases loaded walk to Bradley to make it 4-1.

Porcello settled down and shut out the Rangers from the second through the sixth, despite giving up seven more hits. In the meantime, the Sox got four in the fourth on a single by Bogaerts, run scoring doubles by Ortiz and Ramirez and a two run homer by Holt to go up 5-4. They got one in the sixth on a double by Shaw and a single by Pedroia and added two in the seventh on doubles by Ramirez and Bradley and a run scoring single by Shaw to make it 8-4.

Pedroia led off the seventh with a homer and Odor led off the eighth for Texas with one of his own, it was 9-5. Boston added three in the eighth on a solo homer by Shaw, a double by Leon his fourth hit and third double of the game, and a homer by Betts, his 18th, and the final was 12-5.

Porcello got his 10th win against two losses and Sandy Leon's average went to .500 with 20 hits in 40 at bats since being called up. The Sox had 21 hits including four homers and eight doubles. In addition to Leon's four hits, Bogaerts and Shaw had three each and Betts, Pedroia, Ortiz and Ramirez all had two each.

Baltimore lost to the Dodgers 7-5 so the Sox moved to two games behind the O's in second place.

In Game 2, 8-5 David Price started for the Sox. He immediately gave up a homer to lead off hitter Shin-Soo Choo. Desmond then singled and stole second. Beltre then walked and Rua singled to load the bases, still with no outs. Price then struck out Fielder and Andrus hit a sac fly to right to score Desmond. Price got the last out with no further damage but it was 2-0, Texas, after one inning.

Bradley hit his 14th homer in the second to make it 2-1 but a double by Shaw and a single by Leon were wasted as the Red Sox could not get them in. In the Boston fourth, Holt doubled and Shaw singled. Shaw tried to go to second when the throw went home and was thrown out at second while Holt held at third. With two outs, Betts and Pedroia walked to load the bases and Bogaerts walked to force in Holt to tie the game at 2-2. Ortiz then bounced out to second to end the inning.

The Rangers retook the lead in the sixth when Andrus singled and scored on a double to center by Odor, making it 3-2. It stayed that way until the ninth, when Kimbrel came in for the Sox and walked Andrus, gave up a single to Odor and a run scoring single to Profar. Robinson Chirinos then hit a three run homer to left making it 7-2, still with no outs. Hembree relieved Kimbrel and got the next three batters in succession.

The Sox did not score in the ninth and lost 7-2 with Price, who went eight innings, giving up only three runs on eight hits, while striking out 10, getting his sixth loss. Despite getting 11 hits and five walks, Boston could score only two runs while leaving 14 runners stranded.

The Sox fell into third place, three games behind Baltimore who beat the Dodgers, 4-1, and one half game behind Toronto, who beat the Royals, 8-3, to move into second place.

Trying to win the series, the Sox started Steven Wright against Texas in Game 3. They got off to a quick start in the first when Bogaerts singled to center with two out and Ortiz hit his 20th homer to right center to make it 2-0. Texas got one back in the second when Pedroia made a throwing error allowing Beltre to reach second, Fielder was hit by a pitch and Mazara singled Beltre in to make it 2-1.

Boston loaded the bases in the second, with no outs, on a walk to Bradley and two successive infield errors allowing Brentz and Shaw to reach base. Hanigan then singled to center driving in two runs. Betts doubled to score Shaw and Pedroia reached on another infield error with Hanigan scoring. Ortiz then hit a sac fly to left, scoring Betts, to make it 7-1.

In the third, Bradley doubled to center, Brentz singled to right to drive him in and Shaw doubled to center, scoring Brentz, and making it 9-1. They added two more in the fourth on a walk to Bogaerts, a double by Ramirez, scoring Bogaerts, and a single by Brentz, scoring Ramirez, and making it 11-1.

The Rangers got back two on a homer by Fielder in the sixth. In the seventh, with Wright still pitching, Wilson walked, Profar singled and Desmond hit a triple to right to score two and Layne replaced Wright on the mound for Boston. He gave up a sac fly to Hoying to make it 11-6 and that was all the scoring.

Wright got his 10th win, making him 10-5. Both Baltimore and Toronto won also, so the Sox remained in third, three games back with the Rays coming in for a three game set prior to the All Star Break.

The Sox picked up twelve year veteran infielder, Aaron Hill, from Milwaukee prior to the Rays series. Hill was expected to fill in at third and, according to John Farrell, give the Red Sox another right handed bat in the infield, supposedly against left handed pitching to alternate with Shaw, a left handed hitter. In Game 1, of the series, with tight hander Chris Archer on the mound for the Rays, Farrell started Hill at third in place of Shaw.

After a day off, O'Sullivan started for the Sox in Game 1 and was staked to a two run lead in the first. Betts walked, Pedroia singled and Bogaerts singled to drive in Betts. Bogaerts was thrown out trying to stretch the single into a double but Bradley drove in Pedroia with a sac fly to make it 2-0.

In the top of the second, Dickerson doubled and Franklin singled him in to make it 2-1 and Forsythe led off the third with a homer and it was 2-2. Ortiz hit his 21st homer of the year, his 524 of his career, to lead off the fifth. Holt then singled and stole second but twisted his ankle sliding into second and was replaced by Brentz. Hill, in his second at bat for the Sox, singled to left to score Brentz and make it 4-2.

In the fifth, the Rays got to O'Sullivan for two more on three singles, a walk and a sac fly before leaving the bases loaded with the score 4-4 after five. In the Sox sixth, Ramirez singled, stole second and scored on a single by Brentz who had stayed in the game after running for Holt. The Sox added a run in the eighth on singles by Bradley, Brentz and another RBI single by Hill to make it 6-4.

Uehara came in to close the ninth and gave up a solo homer to Longoria, his fourth hit of the game, but got Morrison to fly out to Bradley to end the game with the Sox up 6-5. Robbie Ross got the win to make his record 1-1 and Uehara got his third save.

Baltimore lost to the Angels 9-5 and the Sox were two back in third place, one behind the second place Blue Jays.

The Sox announced that Closer Craig Kimbrel had a torn meniscus in his left knee suffered while shagging flies in batting practice the night before and would require surgery and be out three to six weeks. Holt had suffered an ankle sprain on his steal of second in the fourth inning and was day to day. Hanley Ramirez had suffered a contusion when hit by a batted ball and would be out for at least one game.

Blake Swihart was placed on the 60 day disabled list with his left ankle sprain and right handed reliever Noe Ramirez was recalled from Pawtucket.

The Sox announced they had acquired 36 year old Closer Brad Ziegler from the Diamondbacks. Ziegler had been in 36 games with the D'Backs this year with a 2.48 ERA and had converted 18 of 20 save opportunities.

Rick Porcello started Game 2 for the Sox and, after giving up a solo homer to second batter, short stop, Brad Miller, in the first inning, shut out the Rays for the next 6 2/3 innings. The Sox got two in the fourth when Pedroia walked and Bogaerts homered deep to left. They added two more in the fifth when Leon singled, Rays center fielder Souza dropped a Betts' fly ball at the wall and Pedroia singled them both in to make it 4-1.

Barnes pitched a perfect eighth in relief of Porcello and Uehara, despite giving up a lead off single in the ninth, struck out the last two batters for his fourth save and second in two days.

Porcello got his 11th win against two losses and lowered his ERA to 3.66. Baltimore won and Toronto lost so the Sox moved into a tie for second with Toronto, two games behind Baltimore with one game to go before the All Star Break.

David Price finally looked like the David Price the Sox had paid all that money for in Game 3, throwing eight innings of shut out ball while striking out ten as the Red Sox ended the pre All Star Break part of the season with a 4-0 win over Tampa Bay to give them a 7-2 home stand.

Price gave up just four hits, none after the third inning, and walked just one while striking out ten, en route to his ninth win. The Sox got three in the first on a single by Betts, a run scoring double by Pedroia and a two run homer to left by Ortiz, his 22nd of the year. They got one more in the second as Sandy Leon continued his hot hitting with a double and scored on Betts' single to make it 4-0. Leon, who had another hit in the game, was now 23-54 for a .442 average.

The two newest members of the Red Sox, Aaron Hill and Brad Ziegler, were impressive. Hill made a sensational diving catch of a line drive in the eighth and Ziegler relieved Price to start the ninth and got the side in order with two strikeouts.

That was all the scoring for the game and the Sox remained two games back, tied for second with Toronto, behind Baltimore as both the Jays and O's won.

The Red Sox All Star representatives, Ortiz, Betts, Bogaerts, Bradley and Wright were flying to San Diego after the game on a special Jet Blue flight. Craig Kimbrel would not be going as he had surgery scheduled to repair the torn meniscus in his left knee.

John Farrell announced that Eduardo Rodriguez would start the first game of the Yankee series in New York after the break. Since he has been rehabbing and Porcello would be available to start after pitching so well on Saturday, there were questions about why to rush Rodriguez in for the start when everyone else would be rested.

At the All Star Break, Red Sox catcher Sandy Leon, who had played in his first Big League game of the year on June 7, had 25 hits in 55 at bats for a .455 average, the highest average by a batter with 50 or more at bats at the All Star Break in baseball history.

The following article appeared in my column BASEBALL WORLD in the July 10, 2016 edition of the Biddeford Journal Tribune.

FOUR RED SOX TO START IN ALL STAR GAME

For the first time since 2005, the Boston Red Sox are sending four starters to the All Star Game this year. It's really an amazing mix of old and new that the Sox are parading out there.

On the one hand, there are the KILLER BEE'S, Xander Bogaerts, Mookie Betts and Jackie Bradley, as talented a trio of players under the age of 25 as have ever arrived at the same team at the same time. They hold the future of the Red Sox franchise in the palms of their collective hands.

On the other hand, there is David Ortiz, who reminds me of that line of Hunter Thompson's that went ' Life should not be a journey to the grave with the intention of arriving safely in a pretty and well preserved body, but rather to skid in broadside in a cloud of smoke, thoroughly used up, totally worn out and loudly proclaiming 'Wow! What a Ride'. ' Ortiz, who chose to make this his last year playing the game, is doing just that.

Hopefully, his broadside slide will end in a World Series Victory and, knowing David, he already has a place in his trophy room for the World Series Most Valuable Player Trophy.

The last time the Red Sox had four players in the starting lineup for an All Star Game was 2005 when Jason Varitek, Manny Ramirez, Johnny Damon and David Ortiz represented the team. Of course, the Red Sox were reigning World Champs so Terry Francona was the AL Team Manager. Damon led off for the AL, Ortiz hit third and Ramirez cleanup with Varitek in the eighth spot. Ortiz drove in Damon in the third to put the AL up 2-0 in a game they eventually won, 7-5. Varitek batted twice and had a walk and a single in the game played at Comerica Park in Detroit.

Of course, the festivities have already begun for this year's version of the All Star Extravaganza. Tomorrow night the crowd in San Diego will be treated to the fireworks show that is the Home Run Derby. While this is a real crowd pleaser and draws a huge crowd, both in person and on TV, around the world, it bears more resemblance to slow pitch softball than to Major League baseball.

The Game itself, on Tuesday night, is perhaps the greatest of the All Star Games because of the unique individual confrontations that make baseball the most one on one of all the Major Sports. Whether it's the pitcher against the batter, the batter against the fielder, the runner against the fielder or whatever configuration, baseball provides constant competition between individual team members.

It seems that no one, including myself, can talk about the All Star Game these days without bemoaning the fact that the winner determines home field advantage in the World Series. Trying to make the All Star Game more important than an exhibition game, Commissioner Bud Selig proclaimed that the winning team would win home field advantage for its representative in the World Series.

Of course, this decision was reached after the 2002 All Star Game ended in a tie, sending fans into a furor and probably prompting Selig's reaction to save face for the game. While there is obviously an advantage to playing at home in any game, the real advantage in a seven game series is in playing that seventh and deciding game at home. The format has the home team playing games 1 and 2 at home, games 3, 4 and 5 on the road and games 6 and 7 at home. So, if the series goes 5 games, the visiting team actually had home field advantage, if it goes 6, they had equal advantage.

Since only two of the last ten World Series have gone to seven games, this advantage would seem to be miniscule. Baseball tarnishes its own image by pretending that this wonderful parade of the best of the best is anything more than that. It is a meaningless game, as it should be, and, while giving it more meaning may have helped baseball put a better spin on the 2002 debacle, there's no reason to continue the charade.

Every team plays 20 games of its regular schedule against teams from the other league. Some people, myself included, have argued that the World Series home field advantage should go to the team with the best record in Inter-league play. Since 2004, the American League has won more Inter-league games than the National in every year. Perhaps the Designated Hitter rule contributes to this imbalance but for whatever reason this would not appear to be a fair way to make the determination.

Giving the home field advantage to the league that won the previous World Series would not appear to be fair either as the American League has won 64 of the previous 111 World Series and the National only 47.

The bottom line is, almost any solution will have its critics and valid reasons why it should or should not be the way. There are two very simple ways, each of which can be argued for or against, but both of which make more sense that the current method.

Those two methods are; alternate the home field advantage from year to year or make a random selection annually. Maybe the current genius in the Commissioner's Office could schedule a coin flip during the seventh inning stretch at the All Star Game.

Carl H. Johnson
July 10, 2016

CHAPTER 14

THE SECOND HALF BEGINS

JULY 12-27

The All Star Game was played in San Diego's PetCo Park on July 12. The American League's starting lineup had David Ortiz, the designated hitter, batting fourth, Xander Bogaerts, the shortstop, batting fifth, Mookie Betts, the right fielder, batting seventh, and Jackie Bradley, the left fielder, batting ninth.

The American League won the game, 4-2, with a three run inning in the second. Betts doubled and scored a run in that inning and Bradley beat out an infield hit but didn't score. Ortiz walked in the third and Encarnacion ran for him, moved to third on a double by Bogaerts and scored the American League's fourth run. Bradley had another hit making him the only AL player with two hits beside Eric Hosmer of the Royals, who was named MVP. The other Red Sox representative, Steven Wright, did not get into the game.

The Sox traveled to New York to meet the Yankees in a three game series after the All Star Break. After announcing that Eduardo Rodriguez would start Game 1 of the series, Farrell started Steven Wright instead and for five innings, the only baserunner the Yankees had against Wright was Alex Rodriguez who reached on a dribbler down the third base line that went for a hit with two outs in the fifth.

In the meantime, the Sox had gotten to Yankee starter, Michael Pineda on a solo homer by Ryan Hanigan, his first of the year, in the third. They got two more in the top of the fifth when Bradley walked to lead off the inning and Travis Shaw hit his tenth homer deep to right to make it 3-0. In the top of the sixth, Pedroia led off with a single and Bogaerts homered deep to left to make it 5-0. The Sox then loaded the bases with two outs on a single by Ortiz and walks to Shaw and Holt before Hanigan flew out to end the thirty minute inning.

Wright came out for the sixth and had obviously lost control of his knuckler. He was all over the place and gave up a lead off single to Castro and walked the number nine hitter Headley. After Gardner flew out, he walked Ellsbury to load the bases with the three, four hitters coming up. Beltran singled to right to score two and it was obvious to everyone in the ball park, except Farrell, that Wright was done. He left him in, however, and another run scored on a grounder to first when the Sox couldn't turn two on a weak throw from Ramirez trying to get the force at second. Fortunately, the next batter, Teixeira, went after the first pitch and popped out to end the inning with the Sox still up 5-3.

Ziegler came in and had a perfect seventh for his second effective outing since joining the Sox. Robbie Ross, despite giving up two singles, held the Yanks in the eighth and Koji Uehara got Teixeira, Rodriguez and Gregorius in order in the ninth for his third save in three games. Wright got the win to make his record 11-5 with a 2.78 ERA.

The Orioles beat the Rays and the Jays lost to the Athletics so the Sox remained two games out but were alone in second place with a five game winning streak.

Eduardo Rodriguez made his return to the parent club a success by going seven innings in Game 2 against the Yankees and giving up just one run on four hits, while the Sox were winning 5-2. The Sox scored first in the third when Pedroia reached on a fielder's choice while Betts was scoring from third. Gardner homered for the Yankees in the third to make it 1-1.

In the fourth, Bradley and Brentz singled and Leon drove in Bradley with another single and the Sox went up 2-1. With Bradley and Hill on with singles in the sixth, Leon homered to make it 5-1 and give him four RBI's for the game.

Rodriguez left ahead 5-1 after seven and Barnes gave up a lead off homer to Headley to make it 5-2 before retiring the side with no further scoring. Uehara got the Yankees 3, 4 and 5 hitters, Rodriguez, McCann and Teixeira, in order, for the second night in a row, in the ninth and his fourth save in four games.

On Sunday with the Orioles having already lost to Tampa Bay, 5-2, the Sox had the opportunity to complete the sweep of the Yankees by taking Game 3. They started David Price, 9-6, against Masahiro Tanaka, 6-2. With one out in the first, Pedroia took Tanaka deep to left for his ninth homer of the season and a 1-0 lead for the Sox.

Despite a rocky start where he gave up three hits and a walk in the first three innings, Price was still up 1-0 going to the fourth. With two outs and runners on second and third in the fourth, after a single by Gregorius and a double by Castro, he gave up consecutive singles to Romine, Gardner and Ellsbury and the score was 3-1, New York.

That was the scoring for the day as Tanaka made it through six with just three hits and no more runs. New York's Betances, Miller and Chapman, the best back of the bullpen in all of baseball, shut out the Sox with no hits the rest of the way. The Red Sox bats could manage just one single and a double after Pedroia's homer, going hitless in the last four innings. Price left after 5 2/3, giving up 11 hits and striking out just one. He admitted after the game that he had just not had it.

If there was any question about the condition of the rivalry between Boston and New York, the fact that 138,642 fans paid to see the three game series should remove any doubt.

The Sox remained two games behind Baltimore but lost a game to Toronto, now one back of the Sox, after beating Oakland, 5-3. The Red Sox had the next day off before a two game set with the San Francisco Giants in friendly Fenway where they have won 30 of 50 games so far. With 72 games to play, they have only 31 in Fenway and 41 away from home.

The Giants, in first place in the National League West, with the best record in baseball, started ex Red Sox pitcher Jake Peavy in Game 1 against the Sox Rick Porcello. The Sox scored first when Brock Holt hit a solo homer to right with two out in the third. It was Pet Brock Day at Fenway and fans were given a rock with a Red Sox cap to honor Holt before the game.

In the Sox fourth, Pedroia walked and Bogaerts singled to lead off the inning. David Ortiz then hit his 23rd homer of the year and 526th of his career to make it 4-0 Sox.

Porcello went 6 1/3 innings against the Giants, giving up just four hits while holding them scoreless. Ross came in with one on and one out in the seventh and got a double play grounder to end the inning and Ziegler pitched a scoreless eighth. Farrell brought in Uehara in a non-save situation to pitch to left handed slugger Brandon Belt even though left hander Tommy Layne was ready. Uehara struck out Belt but had to be removed because of tightness in his shoulder. Layne came in and got the last two outs of the game and the Sox won 4-0.

Baltimore lost their second straight to the Yankees and the Sox moved to one half game behind them in second place.

Drew Pomeranz started his first game since being acquired by the Sox, in Game 2 against the Giants. He held the Giants scoreless on three hits for three innings while the Sox were scoring three runs, three in the second on a two run homer by Ramirez, his ninth of the year and first in July, with Ortiz on, and a solo homer by Shaw. In the fourth, the Sox unloaded on Giant starter Matt Cain, just back from the disabled list, when Bogaerts led off with a single, Ramirez hit his second two run homer, Bradley doubled, Leon tripled and Holt and Betts doubled back to back to make it 8-0.

Pomeranz came out for the fourth, after a 25 minute break while the Sox were scoring, and gave up a walk and a single and a three run homer to Williamson. Green then singled and Brown hit a two run homer and it was 8-5. After Span beat out a bunt single for the seventh successive batter to reach base, Farrell finally removed Pomeranz. Robbie Ross came in and got the next three batters to end the inning at 8-5. In the Giants fifth, after getting two out, Ross walked Green and Hembree replaced Ross. The next three batters singled, scoring two runs before Hembree finally got Pagan to pop out to end the inning with the Sox lead just 8-7 after five.

After Tommy Layne relieved Hembree to start the sixth and loaded the bases with no outs on a walk and two singles, Barnes came in and got out of the inning with no scoring and held the Giants scoreless through the eighth. In the Sox sixth, Ramirez hit his third two run homer of the game with Ortiz, who had singled, on base, and it was 10-7. Leon led off the eighth with a solo homer and the score was 11-7. He was 2-4 on the night, and raised his average to .435.

Ziegler pitched a perfect ninth for Boston and Barnes got the win. The Sox got 16 hits in the 11-7 win, including Ramirez's three homers, three hits by Betts, including two doubles, and two hits apiece by Bogaerts, Bradley, Leon and Holt. After Pomeranz was removed, the Sox used five relievers to get through the game, depleting the bullpen.

Baltimore lost to the Yankees again, 5-0, to drop ½ game behind the now first place Sox. The Minnesota Twins, with the worst record in the American League, 35-59, were coming in to Fenway for a four game series starting Thursday.

Mookie Betts hit Twins starter, Tyler Duffy's first pitch of Game 1 over the Green Monster and, as Red Barber used to say, it was 'Katie bar the door, as the Sox unloaded on four Twins pitchers for 13 runs on 17 hits to win 13-2. It was the fourth time Betts had led off a game with a homer this year and the sixth of his career. While the offense was delivering three homers and five doubles, Steven Wright was throwing eight innings of four hit ball, giving up just two runs, only one earned, for his 12th victory and lowering his ERA to 2.67.

Wright was perfect for the first 4 1/3 innings before giving up a single to Kepler. The first four hitters in the Red Sox lineup, Betts, Pedroia, Bogaerts and Ortiz, combined for 14 of the hits, with Pedroia going five for five for the fourth time in his career and the other three getting three hits apiece. In addition to Betts' homer, Bradley had one in the fifth and Ortiz got his 24th of the year and 527th of his career in the eighth.

The Orioles beat New York, 4-1, to stay one half game behind the Sox who were 1 ½ games ahead of third place Toronto. Boston had now won nine of its last 10 games and was now 15 games over .500.

For the second night in a row, Mookie Betts led off the game with a homer, this time on the second pitch of the game. It was the second time this year that Betts had led off consecutive games with homers after doing it against Baltimore on May 31 and June 1.

Pedroia struck out after Betts hit his blast but reached on a wild pitch and Bogaerts followed with a single to left and it looked like the Red Sox offense was off again. Ortiz then hit into a 3-6-1 double play and Ramirez lined out to right and that was the end of the Red Sox offense for the next seven innings.

Minnesota starter, Kyle Gibson, held the Sox to a single walk and no more hits through the eighth. Sandy Leon was the only other base runner through the eighth, reaching on an error by third baseman Sano with two out in the eighth.

Brian Dozier hit his 17th homer off Red Sox starter Eddie Rodriguez to lead off the second and it was 1-1 after five. In the sixth, Rodriguez, who had looked good through five, walked Mauer and Farrell removed him after only 95 pitches, one run and six hits. Heath Hembree came in and walked Dozier, then gave up a double to Sano, scoring Mauer, and it was 2-1. It would stay that way, with Ross, Tazawa and Layne holding the Twins scoreless, until the ninth.

The Sox loaded the bases with no outs on singles by Betts and Pedroia and a walk to Bogaerts. With Ortiz and Ramirez due up, it looked like the Sox would pull it out, but Ortiz bounced one to Dozier at second, who threw home for the force on Betts and then catcher Centeno threw to first and got Ortiz for the double play. Hanley Ramirez lined out hard to right for the final out and the Sox had lost 2-1 on just four hits.

Betts was removed from the game in the fifth with soreness in his knee but there appeared to be no structural damage. Tazawa, returning from the disabled list, gave up two singles while holding the O's scoreless in the eighth.

Baltimore had beaten Cleveland 5-1 so the Sox fell back into second place, one half game behind the O's.

After losing Game 2 to the hapless Twins when their offense disappeared, the Sox started David Price in Game 3. After 1 ½ innings they were down 4-1 after Price gave up a windblown triple in the first inning to Grossman, who scored on a sac fly by Dozier and, in the second, singles by Rosario, Buxton and Kepler around a double by Suzuki got them three more. The Sox had gotten one in the first when Ortiz hit a sac fly to score Holt.

In the last of the second, the Sox got five to go up 6-4. Martinez walked, Holt singled, Pedroia doubled to score them and Ortiz walked. Martinez then hit a three run homer to take the lead. The Sox added one in the fourth when Bradley doubled in Ortiz who had reached on a single. The Twins got another in the sixth to make it 7-5, Boston, and knock Price out of the game. An RBI single in the last of the sixth by Bradley made it 8-5, Boston.

Buchholz had come in in relief of Price in the sixth and got a strikeout to get out of the inning. In the seventh, with a man on first and two outs, Kepler hit a fly to right that Michael Martinez

misplayed into a triple, scoring one run. The next batter, Vargas, hit a blooper down the left field line that neither Bogaerts nor Holt, in left, could catch and it fell for a double, making it 8-7.
Farrell brought in Tommy Layne who gave up a single to Rosario, scoring Vargas and tying the score. Centeno singled and Layne walked Buxton to load the bases. Heath Hembree came in to pitch to Nunez and gave up a ground ball single up the middle, scoring two and making it 10-8 Twins before getting the last out of the inning.

In the last of the seventh, Ortiz doubled in Pedroia who had singled and it was 10-9. Hembree gave up a lead off homer to Sano in the eighth and it was 11-9, Minnesota. After Dozier doubled, Ross relieved Hembree and got the Twins with no further scoring. The Twins bull pen held the Sox scoreless in the eighth and ninth and the final was 11-9.

Ziegler pitched a scoreless inning for the Sox in the ninth. Buchholz, Layne and Hembree in relief, gave up six runs between them and Layne took the loss, his first. The Sox scored nine runs on 15 hits and couldn't win the game. Bogaerts got four hits and Ortiz and Bradley got three each.

In addition to the disappointing loss, the Orioles had beaten Cleveland, 5-2, to go 1 ½ games up on the second place Sox. Price had another disappointing outing, going just 5 2/3 innings and giving up five runs on 11 hits and raising his ERA to 4.51.

Porcello started for Boston in Game 4 as the Sox tried for a split of the four games. Bogaerts booted a grounder to start the second and Porcello walked Vargas and gave up a two run double to the eighth hitter, catcher Centeno and it was 2-0, Twins. The Sox got three in the third on singles by Pedroia and Bogaerts and a three run homer by Ramirez, his 13th, to go up 3-2. In the Twins fourth, Kepler tripled and scored on a ground out to tie it at 3-3.

In the fifth, the Sox unloaded on Twins' starter Tommie Milone. Pedroia hit a solo homer with one out and Bogaerts and Ramirez followed with singles. After Bradley struck out, Hill reached on a grounder through third baseman Sano to score Bogaerts. Shaw then hit his 12th homer to right to score three and make it 8-3 Boston.

In the Twins' seventh, Vargas doubled and, with one out, Holt lost a fly off the bat of Centeno in the sun and, when he dropped it, the scorer gave Centeno a double, leaving runners on second and third. Buxton then singled in the two runners and it was 8-5. With two outs, Barnes relieved Porcello and got the last out with no further problems.

In the Twins' eighth, Barnes loaded the bases with no outs on two singles and a walk and was relieved by Tazawa who gave up a sac fly for one run and a single to Centeno for another and it was 8-7 after eight.

Ziegler, who was now the Sox' Closer, came in for the ninth and got the first three hitters in the Twins lineup, Nunez, Mauer and Sano, in order with two strikeouts and earned the save, his first as a member of the Red Sox and his 19th of the year between Arizona and Boston. He had now been in six games and pitched six innings without giving up a run and had allowed only one hit.

Bogaerts had another three hit game, making him 21 for 32 against Minnesota this year, a .656 average. Pedroia and Ramirez each had two hits. Porcello got his 13th win against two losses.

Baltimore stayed 1½ games ahead of the Sox by beating Cleveland again, 5-3. The Detroit Tigers were coming in the next day, Monday, July 25th, for a three game series to end the home stand.

Justin Verlander started Game 1 for the Tigers while Drew Pomeranz made his second start for the Sox. Boston scored first in the bottom of the second on a single by Bradley and an RBI double by Shaw. At the end of five, it was still 1-0, Boston and Pomeranz had given up just two hits while striking out seven. In the top of the sixth, Romine singled and, after one out, former Red Sox shortstop Jose Iglesias homered to put the Tigers up 2-1.

Joe Kelly, just back from rehab in Pawtucket, relieved Pomeranz and gave up a triple to deep center by Upton who then scored on a single by McCann to make it 3-1. Buchholz came on for the eighth and gave up a lead off single to Iglesias, who went to second on a passed ball, to third on a fly out to right and scored on Martinez' single to center to make it 4-1.

The Sox loaded the bases in the eighth on singles by Ortiz, Martinez and Bradley with no outs. After Brentz, hitting for Shaw, struck out, Leon singled to center to drive in Ortiz and make it 4-2 with one out and the bases loaded. After Holt struck out for the second out, Francisco Rodriguez came in in relief of Wilson, the Tigers third pitcher, and got Betts to hit into a force play to end the inning with Boston still behind, 4-2.

Rodriguez shut down the Sox in order in the ninth to get the save. Verlander, who had gone six innings, giving up just one run on five hits, got his 10th win and Pomeranz got his eighth loss against eight wins although he had a quality start, going six innings and giving up just two runs on four hits.

Baltimore beat Colorado 3-2 to move to 2 ½ games ahead of Boston and three ahead of third place Toronto.

The Tigers got four runs in the first two innings against Steven Wright in Game 2. In the first, former Red Sox shortstop Jose Iglesias singled and Miguel Cabrera hit a homer deep to right to make it 2-0. In the second, another former Red Sox player Mike Aviles, singled and went to second on a wild pitch and scored on a single by Collins. Collins then stole second and scored on another single by Iglesias and it was 4-0.

In the third, Mookie Betts got a double, his first of two in the game, Bogaerts was hit by a pitch and Ortiz hit his 25th homer of the season and 528th of his career to make it 4-3. In the fourth, a walk to Bradley, single by Shaw and another double by Betts put the Sox up 5-4.

In the top of the fifth, Wright walked the first two batters, gave up a run scoring single to Victor Martinez and a single to Casetllanos, loading the bases with no outs. Upton then grounded out to Ramirez at first with another run scoring. With two outs, another former Red Sox player, Jarred Saltalamacchia singled to drive in two more and make it 8-5, Detroit.

In the sixth, Bradley led off with a homer. Leon was then hit with a pitch, Holt reached on an error on a grounder to Kinsler at second and Betts walked to load the bases with one out. Pedroia then singled to drive in Leon and Holt scored when Bogaerts hit into a force out and the game was tied at 8-8.

In the seventh, Robbie Ross, who had relieved Wright in the fifth, got the first two outs but then hit Upton, gave up a single to Aviles and walked Saltalamacchia to load the bases. He then walked Collins to force in the go ahead run, making it 9-8. Joe Kelly relieved Ross and got Kinsler to fly out to end the inning.

The Sox were shut down the rest of the way by Rondon, Greene and Rodriguez, who worked an inning apiece. Rodriguez got the save for Detroit, his second in two nights and his 29th of the year. Ross got the loss, making him 1-2. Steven Wright lasted just 4 2/3 innings, giving up eight runs on nine hits in what was probably his worst outing of the year and saw his ERA balloon to 3.12.

Baltimore lost to Colorado 6-3 while Toronto was beating San Diego 7-6 to move back into second place, 2 ½ games behind Baltimore and ½ game ahead of the third place Sox.

Trying to salvage one game of the series, the Sox started Eduardo Rodriguez against Detroit in Game 3. Pedroia got them off quickly with a solo homer to center in the first. In the Detroit third, Kinsler reached on an infield single, Iglesias doubled and

Cabrera was walked intentionally to set up the double play. Victor Martinez then singled in Kinsler and Iglesias and it was 2-1, Detroit. In the sixth, Rodriguez gave up a solo homer to McCann and, when he walked Collins, was replaced by Barnes, who got out of the inning with the score 3-1, Tigers.

Bogaerts hit a lead off homer to left center to lead off the Boston seventh and make it 3-2. In the eighth, Shaw singled to left and Leon sacrificed him to second. Betts then tripled to deep center, scoring Shaw with the tying run. Rondon replaced starter Fulmer and struck out Pedroia to end the inning.

With the score still 3-3 in the top of the ninth, Ziegler came in to pitch for Boston. He got the first two outs but Miguel Cabrera homered with two outs and it was 4-3, Detroit, going to the last of the ninth. It was the first run Ziegler had given up in seven appearances for the Sox.

Justin Wilson came in to pitch the ninth for Detroit and got Bogaerts, Ortiz and Bradley in order for his first save and the Tigers had swept the Red Sox. Rodriguez lasted just 5 1/3 innings, giving up three runs on nine hits and striking out six and Ziegler got the loss, his fourth against two wins between Boston and Arizona.

They had now lost six of their last ten and were starting an 11 game road trip to the west coast the next day. Toronto lost to San Diego, 8-4, and Baltimore lost to Colorado, 3-1, so the Sox remained in third place.

CHAPTER 15

THE TRIP WEST

JULY 28-AUGUST 7

The Sox finally got a performance worthy of his $23. million a year salary out of David Price in Game 1 at Los Angeles and could do nothing to back it up. Price went eight shut out innings, giving up seven hits and striking out six and left ahead 1-0 after eight. The only run had been scored in the third when Sandy Leon had singled, gone to third on a single to right by Brock Holt and scored on a sac fly to left by Mookie Betts. It was Betts' 66th RBI the most by a lead off hitter in all of baseball.

In the last of the ninth, Brad Ziegler came in to pitch and Mike Trout and Albert Pujols singled to start the inning. After a failed sacrifice ended in a strikeout, Andrelton Simmons singled to load the bases with one out. Former Red Sox player Daniel Nava hit a chopper to Hanley Ramirez at first and he threw home to try for the force out. The throw went wild and two runs scored ending the game 2-1 Angels.

Ziegler got the loss in his second successive poor performance, even though the runs were unearned, he had set it up. Price's ERA improved to 4.26 and the performance was encouraging. The Red Sox could manage just eight singles against the Angels pitchers.

After getting a strong performance out of Price, it was a discouraging loss for the Sox in the first game of the western swing. However, Baltimore lost to Minnesota 6-2, so they did not lose any ground on first place.

Rick Porcello, with his 13-2 record, started Game 2 for the Sox and pitched a gem. He went all the way, giving up just two runs on five hits while the Sox were scoring six against Angels' starter Tim Lincecum and the bullpen.

The Angels got their two in the second when Pujols singled and Nava doubled to put runners on second and third. Pujols scored when Simmons grounded to short and Perez singled to center to score Nava. That put them up 2-0 but that was all they'd get.

In the meantime, Boston got two in the third. Betts walked and stole second. Pedroia walked but Betts was then thrown out trying to steal third. Bogaerts doubled to center, scoring Pedroia, and Ortiz singled to center to score Bogaerts. Ramirez walked but Lincecum got Bradley to fly out to center for the third out. In the fourth, Hill singled to center, Hanigan walked and Holt singled to right to load the bases. Betts then drove in Hill with a sac fly to center and Pedroia grounded into a 6-4-3 double play to end the inning with the Sox up, 3-2.

Bradley led off the sixth with a homer to right, his 17th, and Bogaerts homered in the seventh, his 13th, with Pedroia, who had singled, on base, to make the final 6-2. Porcello, threw 107 pitches, 81 for strikes, in gaining his 14th win, tying him for first in the American League in wins. Bogaerts went 2-5 with three RBI's and raised his average to .331 and his RBI total to 66. The Sox now had five players with 60 or more RBI's with Ortiz at 85, second in the league behind Toronto's Encarnacion, Betts, 67, Bradley, 62 and Ramirez, 60, more players than any other team in baseball.

The Sox remained in third place, 1 ½ games back, as Toronto beat Baltimore, 6-5, to move to ½ game behind the O's. On Saturday afternoon, before the Sox game, Toronto beat Baltimore 9-1 to move into first place with the Sox still 1 ½ game down but with the opportunity to gain ½ game with a win in Game 3 against Los Angeles on Saturday night.

Once again, the Red Sox got off to a quick start in Game 3. Betts hit a lead off homer, his 6th to lea doff a game this year and his 21st homer of the season. After Betts' blast, Angels' starter, Hector Santiago walked Pedroia and Bogaerts and, after Bradley, batting cleanup for the first time in his Major League career, struck out,

Ramirez singled home Pedroia. With two outs, Shaw walked to load the bases but Brentz looked at a called third strike and it was 2-0.

In the last of the first, with Pomeranz on the hill for the Sox, Trout and Pujols singled, moved to second and third on a wild pitch and Trout scored on Marte's ground out and it was 2-1. In the top of the third, the Sox loaded the bases again on a single by Bogaerts and walks to Bradley and Shaw before Brentz took another called third strike to end the threat.

In the last of the third, Escobar walked and Pujols homered to make it 3-2, Angels. Giavatella singled in Simmons who had doubled in the Angels' fourth to make it 4-2. When Pomeranz walked Simmons with one out in the sixth, Kelly replaced him and gave up a double to Brandy, scoring Simmons with the last run of the game and the final was 5-2. Kelly pitched 2 1/3 innings in relief, giving up just one more hit.

In addition to leaving the bases loaded twice in the first three innings, the Sox had runners on first and second with one out in the fourth and didn't score and runners on first and second with two outs in the sixth and didn't score. Santiago got the win after a rocky five innings in which he threw 119 pitches but was able to get out of trouble time after time.

Pomeranz got the loss, making his record 8-9 with a 3.05 ERA. The Sox were in third place, two games behind first place Toronto and, despite losing two of the first three to the Angels, had gained a ½ game on first place since the series started.

Game 4 started with Steven Wright on the mound for the Sox and Tyler Skaggs, making his second start in two years after Tommy John surgery, for the Angels.

In one of the strangest first innings ever seen, Wright gave up a lea doff double to Escobar and then walked Calhoun. Trout then singled to left and, when Escobar tried to score, Brentz threw a strike from left field to home but Hanigan dropped the ball trying to tag him. As Hanigan missed the ball, Escobar slid past home without touching it. Wright picked up the ball and tagged Escobar out. Pujols then hit a little pop up that fell in right and the bases were loaded with one out.

Wright then struck out Simmons but when the third strike got by Hanigan, Calhoun tried to score from third and Hanigan threw to Wright covering home and he tagged Calhoun out. Wright had gotten two put outs at the plate and struck out a batter in the inning while giving up three hits and a walk but allowing no runs.

In the third inning, Trout hit a shot that caught Wright on his pitching forearm but he was able to continue. It was 0-0 after four as the Sox could do nothing with Skaggs who had only given up two hits. In the last of the fourth, with one out, singles by Escobar, Calhoun and Trout, scoring Escobar, a ground out by Pujols driving in Calhoun and a single by Marte driving in Trout made it 3-0, Angels.

Buchholz replaced Wright at the start of the sixth and held the Angels to no runs and one hit for three innings. Skaggs lasted 5 1/3 innings, giving up just four hits and no runs. His relief held the Sox scoreless and the game went to the top of the ninth 3-0, Angels.

The Red Sox offense had done nothing all day and Angels' Closer, Houston Street, came on for the ninth. Bradley walked to lead off the inning and Hill singled to center. Hanigan, a right handed batter, was allowed to hit for himself against the right hander Street with both Leon, a switch hitter, and Shaw, a leftie, available. Hanigan was hitting .165 and was in an 0-16 streak. Street struck him out and also fanned Holt to make it two out.

Betts then singled to right to score Bradley and make it 3-1 with two on and two outs. Dustin Pedroia hit 1-0 pitch for a three run homer to straight away center to put the Sox up 4-3 and Bogaerts capped the unbelievable rally with a homer to left, making it 5-3.

Ziegler came in for the last of the ninth and got one out. He then gave up a single to Escobar, his third hit of the game, but then got Calhoun to ground to second. Pedroia fielded the grounder, tagged Escobar and threw to first for the double play and the Sox had one of the most exciting come from behind victories in memory.

Buchholz got the win, making him 4-9 and Ziegler got his 20th save. The game winner was Pedroia's 12th of the year and Bogaerts' homer was his 14th.

Baltimore beat Toronto, 6-2, in twelve innings, to move back into first with Toronto one game back and the Sox just 1 ½ behind in third. The Sox had managed only a split with the Angels but had gained a half game on first place in doing so. They now traveled to Seattle for a four game series with the Mariners who were 51-49, in third place in the West, six games behind the Texas Rangers.

The trading deadline came and went on the afternoon of Monday, August 1, with rumors swirling all day that Dave Dombrowski was trying to engineer a deal for Chris Sale, the White Sox Ace, who was 14-4. Sources were speculating about how much of their young talent the Red Sox would be willing to surrender to get Sale.

Sale had been the center of controversy in Chicago in April, openly and publicly critical of White Sox management for the banning of Adam La Roche's son from the clubhouse which La Roche claimed caused his early retirement. Just a short time ago, Sale was suspended for cutting up the team's retro uniforms because he didn't want to wear them in a game. Red Sox fans were sure that Sale would be the last piece of the Red Sox World Series puzzle if they could get him. With the Red Sox 1 ½ game out of first place and the young team working so well together, I did not feel that introducing a potential trouble maker like Sale to the positive Sox environment would be a productive, no matter how good he was.

At any rate, the deadline came and went without Sale coming to Boston. Dombrowski did acquire 30 year old, left handed, reliever Fernando Abad from the Minnesota Twins, giving up right handed reliever Pat Light in the trade. Abad, who was in 39 games at Minnesota this year, with a 2.95 ERA will bolster the Sox bull pen, giving them a left hander who has held left handed hitters to a .163 average this year.

Eduardo Rodriguez started Game 1 at Seattle against the Mariners James Paxton. For six innings, Rodriguez and Paxton were 0-0, with Rodriguez giving up just one hit. In the Seattle seventh, Robinson Cano doubled and Nelson Cruz walked. Dae-Ho Lee then doubled to center to score Cano and leave runners on second and third. Robbie Ross came in in relief and hit the first batter, Kyle Seager, to load the bases. He then struck out Franklin Gutierrez and Chris Iannetta to end the inning with the Sox down 1-0.

In the Sox eighth, with one out, Aaron Hill hit a homer to left, his first since joining the Red Sox and, after Tazawa pitched a rocky, but scoreless eighth, it went to the ninth 1-1. In the top of the ninth, Seattle brought in Closer Steve Cishek and the lead off hitter Mookie Betts hit his second pitch over the left field wall to put the Sox up 2-1.

Craig Kimbrel, just off the disabled list, came in to pitch the ninth for the Sox. He got the first hitter on a come backer to the mound. He then struck out Seager, but when the third strike got away from catcher Sandy Leon, Seager reached base. He struck out pinch hitter Adam Lind for the second out but then walked pinch hitter Michael Zunino to put the tying run on second, with two outs. He struck out Shawn O'Malley for the last out and the Red Sox had come from behind to win two nights in a row.

Rodriguez had his best game of the season, giving up just the one run on three hits and striking out six while walking two. Seattle's Paxton went eight and gave up one run on four hits. The win went to Tazawa, who pitched the eighth and Kimbrel got his 18th save. Boston could manage only two hits beside the two home runs in squeaking out the win.

The Sox moved back into second place, just one game behind the O's, who did not play, and one percentage point ahead of third place Toronto, who lost to Houston 2-1.

After the game, the Red Sox announced that 22 year old Andrew Benintendi, their highly touted outfield prospect, who was hitting .295 at Portland, would join the team in Seattle the next day. Benintendi, rated the Sox second best prospect behind infielder Yoan Moncada, was rated the 15th best prospect in all of baseball by Baseball America. Moncada is hitting .289 at Portland and was felt a good bet to make the Sox either later this year or next year. Both had been mentioned as possible trade bait in the effort to acquire Chris Sale but it appeared that Dombrowski did not want to give up the future for Sale.

David Price started Game 2 for the Sox and held the Mariners scoreless on just three hits for seven innings. In the meantime, the Sox had gotten a run in the first as Ortiz doubled to left with two outs to drive in Pedroia, who had walked. They added two in the fourth on a solo homer to left center by Ramirez, his 14th of the year, and an RBI single by Hill, driving in Bradley who had doubled. They made it 4-0 in the top of the eighth when Betts doubled, went to third when Pedroia grounded to second and scored when Ortiz flew out to left. It was Ortiz's 87th RBI of the year.

After pitching so well for seven innings, Price gave up a lea doff homer to Mike Zunino in the eighth and Leonis Martin, Luis Sardinas and Guillermoa Heredia got consecutive singles, scoring the second run and knocking Price out with runners in first and second and no one out and the score 4-2. Barnes came in and struck out pinch hitter Seth Smith.

Left hander Fernando Abad then came in in relief of Barnes to pitch to left hander Robinson Cano in his first appearance for the

Sox since being acquired from the Twins. On a 1-2 pitch, Cano hit his 24th homer of the year to right center field and the Mariners were up 5-4.

In the Sox ninth, Edwin Diaz took over on the mound for Seattle. He struck out Bradley, walked Shaw and struck out Leon. With two outs, Andrew Benintendi, who had pinch hit for Brentz in the seventh and stayed in to play left field, in his first big league game, struck out for the third out and the Sox had blown a 4-0 lead and lost 5-4.

Abad took the loss making his record between the Twins and Boston 1-5, not an auspicious debut. Price had pitched well and had only thrown 98 pitches when he came out and got no decision. His record remained 9-7 in 23 starts and his ERA was 4.30.

With the loss, the Sox record slipped to 58-47 and they fell two games behind first place Baltimore, who beat Texas 5-1 and one game behind second place Toronto who beat Houston 2-1.

Rick Porcello, 14-2, took the mound in Game 3. He gave up lead off home runs in the second and sixth to Nelson Cruz and Mike Zunino and a two out homer to Adam Lind in the seventh and only one other hit in eight innings. Unfortunately, the Sox could do nothing with Mariner starter Hisashi Iakuma, who gave up five hits and no runs through 7 1/3, or reliever Drew Storen who replaced him and got out of the eighth with the score 3-0.

For the second night in a row, Edwin Diaz came in to pitch the ninth for Seattle. He struck out Ortiz and gave up a single to Bradley. He then hit Hill with a pitch and a wild pitch put the runners on second and third with one out. Shaw then grounded to second for the second out, scoring Bradley. Diaz got Leon to ground to second and the Sox had lost 3-1.

Despite a fine performance, Porcello got his third loss, striking out eight and walking just one in throwing the complete game.

Andrew Benintendi, getting his first start in left field, got two of Boston's seven hits, singles in the third and eighth. Diaz got his second save in two nights against the Sox.

Baltimore beat Texas, 3-2, and Toronto bested Houston 3-1, so Boston fell to three behind the Orioles with the last game in Seattle coming up before the three in Los Angeles against the Dodgers. The Sox were now 3-4 on the west coast trip.

Pomeranz started for the Sox in Game 4 and went six innings, leaving with the score tied at 2-2. It was his best start since joining the Sox as he gave up just two runs on four hits despite walking six batters.

The Sox had scored first on a homer by Shaw in the second. They got another in the fifth when Brentz and Betts got back to back doubles to make it 2-0 with Betts on second and nobody out. However, Seattle starter Ariel Miranda got Bogaerts, Ortiz and Pedroia without further scoring.

In the last of the fifth, Shawn O'Malley hit a lead off homer to left to make it 2-1. Heredia then reached on a drag bunt and went to third on two ground outs. After Cruz was walked intentionally, Dae-Ho Lee singled to center to drive in Heredia with the tying run.

The game went to the ninth tied 2-2 and Abad came in for his second relief appearance with the Sox. O'Malley singled with one out and with two outs, Abad walked Gutierrez to put the tying run on second with Cano coming up. Farrell brought in Kimbrel to relieve Abad and he got Cano to ground out and send the game to extra innings.

Neither team could score in the tenth and Shaw led off the Boston 11th with a ground single to left. Leon sacrificed him to second and Holt hit a ground ball single which was deflected by shortstop O'Malley allowing Shaw to score. Ziegler came in for the bottom of the 11th and walked Zunino who was then sacrificed to second by Martin and went to third when O'Malley grounded out to first. Seth Smith came in to pinch hit and, for the second night in a row, struck out, ending the game 3-2, Boston.

Kimbrel got the win, his second with three losses and Ziegler got his 21st save. Tazawa and Ross pitched scoreless innings in the seventh and eighth. Pomeranz lowered his ERA to 3.09 but got no decision.

Texas beat Baltimore 5-3 and Toronto beat Houston 4-1, so Toronto moved into a virtual tie with the O's in first while the Red Sox were in third, just two games back.

The following article appeared in my blog on August 5, 2016 at baseballworldbjt.com.

SOX LOST HITTING, FOUND PITCHING

The Red Sox start a three game series with the Los Angeles Dodgers tonight on the west coast. They have been out west since July 28, splitting a four game series with the Angels in Anaheim and doing the same with the Mariners in Seattle.

They have won four and lost four at the beginning of this 11 game trip. Everyone in Red Sox land has been complaining about their terrible remaining schedule which includes another long western swing later in the season.

The Red Sox had averaged 5.68 runs per game overall and 4.62 per game on the road in the 99 games prior to starting this trip. Since they have been on the west coast, they have played eight games and scored a total of 24 runs or three per game.

Fortunately for the Sox, their starting pitching, presently a five man rotation that includes David Price, Rick Porcello, Steven Wright, Eduardo Rodriguez and Drew Pomeranz, has given up just 23 runs in that period. The starters earned run average for that stretch is 3.32. The team ERA for the year is 4.30, 18th worst in all of baseball but the starters have stepped up on this trip.

Even in games that they have lost, the starting pitching has been effective. Porcello, who had only pitched four complete games in his entire career, has pitched two complete games in a row, although he lost one. Price has looked like the old David Price, except for that one inning in Seattle. Rodriguez had his best outing of the year in Game 1 at Seattle.

If the starting pitching hadn't stepped up on this trip, the Red Sox would not have been able to split eight games. When the trip started, the Sox were in third place 2 ½ games behind Baltimore. Today, after eight days on the road, they have gained a half game and trail the Orioles and Blue Jays, who are now tied for first, by just two games. While they have seen their bats silenced going from 5.68 runs per game to 3.0, they have actually gained a half game on first place.

Hopefully, the bats will come alive in Los Angeles the next three days. There are 55 games left for the Red Sox to play in this season and they are still in the thick of it. If the starting pitching can continue to do the job as it has in the last eight days, bad schedule or not, and the Sox return to their hitting form, Red Sox fans will be enjoying a longer season than they have the last two years.

Carl H. Johnson
August 5, 2016

Steven Wright started the first game in Los Angeles for Boston in front of 52,728 fans in Dodger Stadium. His knuckleball was at its best as he pitched the first complete game shut out of his career, giving the Dodgers just three hits, striking out nine and walking just one batter. After giving up a double to Turner in the first inning, he retired 19 of the next 20 batters including 15 in a row from the third to the seventh inning.

While the Red Sox streak of quality starting pitching was continuing, the Sox were scoring nine runs on 10 hits, including three homers. The scoring started in the second, when Ramirez walked and was forced at second when Bradley grounded to third. Hill then singled to center, sending Bradley to third and he scored when Leon hit a sac fly to left, making it 1-0. They added another when Betts hit a homer, his 23rd, to left, in the third.

In the fourth, with two out, Hill walked and Leon hit a home run to left, his 4th, to make it 4-0. It stayed that way until the eighth when Shaw hit a lead off homer. Bogaerts and Bradley then singled and Hill was walked intentionally to load the bases. Leon then singled to drive in Bogaerts, his fourth RBI of the game and, when Chase Utley mishandled a grounder by Holt on a force attempt, both Bradley and Hill scored. Betts then singled to drive in Leon, his second RBI of the game and his 73rd of the season, which leads all lead off hitters, to make the final 9-0 .

Wright's masterful performance improved his record to 13-5 and lowered his ERA to 3.01. He threw 119 pitches, 78 for strikes. Playing in the National League park with no DH, David Ortiz did not play. Pedroia had to leave the game in the fourth when he fouled a ball off his left shin causing a contusion but tests were negative and he was listed as day to day. Hill moved to second to replace him and Shaw took over for Hill at third. Wright did not have as good a night at the plate as he did on the mound, striking out three times in four at bats.

Baltimore defeated the Chicago White Sox, 7-5, and Toronto edged the Kansas City Royals, 4-3, to stay tied for first and the Sox stayed two games back in third.

In Game 2, the Red Sox bats were silenced again. Two young Dodger hurlers, starter Ross Stripling and reliever Grant Dayton held them scoreless on four hits for seven innings, while the Dodgers were able to score three runs against Boston starter Eduardo Rodriguez who lasted just 4 1/3 innings.

The Dodgers got one in the second on singles by former Red Sox player Adrian Gonzalez, Enrique Henderson and A. J. Ellis. They added two in the fifth when pinch hitter Chris Taylor singled to lead off the inning and Howie Kendrick walked. Corey Seager then doubled to score Taylor and Gonzalez got his third hit of the game, a bloop single, to score Kendrick and it was 3-0.

That would be the final as Barnes, Ross and Buchholz shut the Dodgers down the rest of the way and, after Stripling and Dayton got through seven scoreless, Joe Blanton and Closer Kenley Jansen shut the Sox down in the eighth and ninth.

The Sox could manage only five hits and had 11 strike outs. Their only threat and the only time they had more than one runner on base in an inning was the first when Betts and Holt, playing second for Pedroia who was given the day off to nurse his bruised leg, singled to lead off the game. After Bogaerts struck out, Ortiz, playing first in the National League park, grounded to second and Bradley walked to load the bases with two out. Leon then bounced back to the pitcher for the third out and, for all intents and purposes, the game was over for the Red Sox offense.

Rodriguez got his fifth loss with only two wins. Stripling's record went to 3-3 and Jansen got his 33rd save in 38 tries.

Trying to win the series with the Dodgers and end the road trip over .500, the Red Sox started Ace David Price in the final game of the trip and the series. They got him a quick lead in the first as

Betts walked, stole second, went to third on a wild pitch and scored on Bogaerts fly out to left to make it 1-0.

They got another off starter Brandon McCarthy in the fourth when, with two out, he walked Holt and new catcher Bryan Holaday, who had been acquired on waivers from Texas, and Benintendi singled to score Holt making it 2-0. McCarthy had walked five and hit a batter in the first four innings as he was unable to get the ball near the plate on some pitches. He threw 65 pitches, 31 for balls before being relieved after Benintendi's single, only the second hit he had given up, both to Benintendi.

In the bottom of the fourth, after facing only 11 batters in the first three innings, Price gave up a lead off homer to Turner followed by a double by Gonzalez. An error by Holt at third and a walk to Grandal loaded the bases and left fielder Rob Segedin, in his second at bat, in his first big league game, hit a double off the center field wall, scoring two and making it 3-2, Dodgers. Price then intentionally walked Fields, hitting for the pitcher, and got Kendrick to hit into a 6-4-3 double play ending the inning.

In the fifth, a walk and a single put Turner on second and Gonzalez on first. Turner scored when Bogaerts threw the ball away trying for a force at second. After two were out, Grandal walked and Segedin singled to right, scoring two, his second hit and third and fourth RBI's of his big league career, but Grandal was thrown out trying to go to third to end the inning with the Dodgers up 6-2.

Mercifully, Farrell removed Price, who had thrown 100 pitches in five innings, and brought in Abad who got through the sixth 1-2-3. In the bottom of the sixth, after Shaw singled, Hill, batting for Holt, doubled to score Shaw and Benintendi got his third hit, a single to right, driving in Hill. Ortiz, hitting for Brentz, walked and Betts singled to left, driving in Benintendi and it was 6-5.

In the seventh, Tazawa replaced Abad and, after getting the first out on a pop out, gave up back to back homers to Gonzalez and

Hernandez to make it 8-5. It was the 200th homer of Gonzalez' career.

That was the final as the last ten Red Sox batters in a row were retired by Dodger pitching. For the second game in a row, Kenley Jansen, the Dodgers Closer, struck out the Red Sox side in order in the ninth. In two games, he faced six batters, striking them all out, on just 26 pitches, 22 of which were strikes.

Price got his eighth loss and had one of his worst performances of the year, giving up six runs, only three earned, on four hits and four walks. The start was Price's third on the road trip and the Sox had lost all three games. The Red Sox defense made three errors which did not help but Price was ineffective again. Jansen got his 34th save of the season for the Dodgers.

Baltimore belted the Chicago White Sox, 10-2 so the Red Sox road trip ended with them in third, three games behind the O's. In losing six of 11 on the road, they had only lost ½ game on first, so the failed trip could have been worse. Hanley Ramirez remained out of the lineup, although he pinch hit and struck out in the ninth. He is suffering from a sore wrist suffered in a fall in the dugout after Game 2 at Seattle.

A total of 151,064 fans watched the three game series and there were many Red Sox fans among the crowds. The Sox headed home to start a three game series with the Yankees at Fenway starting on Tuesday night. On Monday, August 8th, while the Red Sox were idle, the Orioles lost to Oakland 3-2 so the Red Sox gained a half game and came home 2 ½ out of first place, exactly where they were when they left on the west coast trip.

CHAPTER 16

BACK HOME AGAIN

AUGUST 8-14

Rick Porcello got the home stand off to a rocky beginning in Game 1. He gave up five hits and two runs in the first three innings and the Sox were down 2-0 to the Yankees. Doubles by Starling Castro and Chase Headley in the second scored one and a double by Brett Gardner and a single by Brian McCann plated the other in the third.

In the last of the third, Benintendi singled and Betts doubled to put men on second and third with one out against Yankee starter Luis Severino. Pedroia then doubled into the right field corner and it was 2-2.

In the Sox fifth, Leon walked and Benintendi followed with a double high off the wall in straight away center, scoring Leon. The ball appeared to have hit the yellow line separating the Green Monster from stands and, after first being ruled a double, was changed to a homer. After the Yankees requested a replay, it was finally ruled a double and it was 3-2 with Benintendi on second with no outs. After Betts bounced back to the pitcher, Pedroia doubled to right center, scoring Benintendi and Ortiz singled to left, scoring Pedroia and it was 5-2, Sox.

Porcello held the Yanks scoreless from the second through the eighth aided by a great play by Bradley in center. In the seventh, Headley hit a drive off the center field wall which took a crazy bounce and went over Bradley's head into deep right center. Bradley chased the ball down and made a throw while he was spinning around towards third, with what appeared to be both feet off the ground, getting the ball to third on one hop to get Headley who was trying for a triple. It was Bradley's 11th outfield assist of the season.

After two were out, Gary Sanchez reached on an error by Shaw at third and Gardner doubled but Porcello got Ellsbury on a liner to right for the third out. Bradley's throw saved at least one and possibly two runs.

It went to the ninth 5-2 and Kimbrel relieved Porcello. After two were out and Headley, who had walked, was on first, Kimbrel walked three batters in a row to force in a run and leave the bases loaded. Kimbrel could not find the plate and went to three balls on five of the six batter he faced. Farrell brought in Barnes to replace him with the tying run on second and he struck out Mark Teixeira to end the game and get the save.

The 5-3 win moved the Sox to 1 ½ games behind Baltimore, who lost 2-1 to Oakland, and Toronto, who got bombed by Tampa Bay, 10-2.

Porcello improved his record to 15-3 with a 3.40 ERA. It was his 11th win in a row this year at Fenway and the 100th win of his career. He struck out five while walking just one and giving up seven hits and two runs in eight innings. It was the third game in a row he had gone at least eight innings. Benintendi had three hits in three at bats and was now 8-16, batting .500, and looking like he belongs in left field, since joining the Sox straight from AA Portland.

Before Game 2 against the Yankees,   the Sox reported that Steven Wright would not start Game 3 as he had soreness in his shoulder which he had bumped sliding back into second base in Seattle when used as a pinch runner. They also reported that Blake Swihart would require surgery on his injured ankle and would be out for the season.

Pomeranz started for the Sox against Nathan Eovaldi for the Yankees.   Neither team scored in the first but Eovaldi was replaced at the start of the second due to right elbow discomfort. The Yankees brought in Chasen Shreve to relieve him, the first of seven different relievers they would use as Manager Joe Girardi tried to piece together a game.

The Sox loaded the bases with only one out in both the third and fourth innings and only scored one run in each inning. Both runs scored on fielder's choices on ground balls, one by Betts and the other by Benintendi. In the fifth, Pomeranz gave up a lead off homer to Gregorius to make it 2-1. He gave up two singles after the homer but got out of the inning with no further scoring.

In the Sox fifth, Bogaerts walked, Betts, batting third, doubled and Ortiz was walked intentionally to load the bases with no outs. Ramirez flied to shallow left, Bradley fouled to first and Hill, batting for Shaw, struck out and the Sox threat went by the boards. Pomeranz gave up a single to Headley and walked Teixeira with one out in the sixth and was replaced by Buchholz, who got Castro to hit into a double play to end the inning 2-1.

Leon walked to lead off the Sox sixth and Benintendi singled to right. Pedroia then singled to left to drive in Leon and Benintendi went to third and scored when Bogaerts hit a grounder, forcing Pedroia at second. Betts hit a double to deep center and Bogaerts was thrown out on a relay from Ellsbury to Gregorius to Romine at home trying to score. After Ortiz was walked intentionally, for the second time, but Ramirez flied out to end the inning, 4-1, Sox.

Barnes replaced Buchholz to start the seventh and gave up singles to Gregorius, Sanchez and Romine to make it 4-2. Barnes then got Alex Rodriguez, pinch hitting, to fly out and Abad replaced him on the mound. Abad struck out Brett Gardner but Ellsbury and Headley got back to back RBI singles and Tazawa replaced Abad. He walked Teixeira to load the bases and gave up a two run scoring double to Castro to make it 6-4 before getting out of the inning.

In the eighth, Tazawa gave up a lead off homer to Sanchez and walked Romine. Robbie Ross came in and gave up a single to Rob Refsnyder. Before getting out of the inning, Ross gave up a walk and threw three wild pitches, two resulting in runs scoring and the score was 9-4. That was the final as the Sox could manage just one hit in the last three innings.

Abad took the loss, making his record 1-6 and the two teams used 15 pitchers between them, eight for the Yankees and seven for the Sox, the most ever in a nine inning game between the two teams.

Toronto beat Tampa Bay, 7-0, while Baltimore was losing to Oakland, 1-0, putting the Jays in first, one game ahead of the O's and 2 ½ ahead of the third place Sox.

In the final game of the three game series, Eduardo Rodriguez started for the Sox against Michael Pineda. Mookie Betts did not play due to tightness in his right calf. The Sox got one in the first when Ortiz hit a ground rule double to right and scored on a single by Ramirez. The double by Ortiz was his 63rd extra base hit of the year, the most by a player over 40 in baseball history and he accomplished it on August 11th in only the 113th game of the year.

Austin Romine homered for the Yankees in the third to make it 1-1. Ramirez drove in Bogaerts, who had singled, with a double in the fifth for his second RBI of the game and made the score 2-1, Sox.

Rodriguez went seven innings, giving up just three hits and striking out six, and left with the Sox still up 2-1. He threw 93 pitches in 94 degree heat and lasted seven innings for only the second time all year. The other time was on July 16, when he beat the Yankees in New York.

Ziegler, who had not given up an earned run in his last four relief appearances, came in and gave up singles to Sanchez, Hicks and Gardner, a double to Ellsbury, on a ball that Benintendi should have caught but lost in the lights, and three runs to make it 4-2. The Sox, who didn't have a base runner in the sixth, seventh and eighth innings, got a double from Leon and a walk to Benintendi with one out in the ninth but Betances struck out Pedroia and Bogaerts to end the game.

The Sox had lost two of three to the Yankees, who had been sellers at the trading deadline, trading many players for future prospects, including Carlos Beltran, Andrew Miller, Ivan Nova and Aroldis Chapman, trying to build for the future and giving up on this year. Those same Yanks now trailed the Sox by just 3½ games. The Sox also lost half a game to Toronto, who had the day off and Boston was now three games back. Baltimore beat Oakland, 9-6, to move to one half game behind Toronto.

On August 12, the Arizona Diamondbacks came into Fenway for a three game series. The Sox started Ace David Price and the game got off to a bizarre start. The first batter Jean Segura hit a long, routine fly ball to center field. As Jackie Bradley settled under it he lost his footing and fell and the ball dropped. Segura ended up on third with a tainted triple. The next batter, Phil Gosselin, hit a fly into center that looked like it was going to drop but Bradley made a shoe string catch and fired a strike to the plate. Segura had started for the plate but turned and went back to third. Before he could get there, the catcher, Holaday, had relayed the throw to Hill at third and doubled Segura up. As if this were not enough for one inning, Paul Goldschmidt then singled to right and Rickie Weeks hit a homer over the Monster in left and it was 2-0 before the Red Sox swung a bat.

In the last of the first, after Pedroia reached on an error by Segura to start the inning, Patrick Corbin, the D'Back's starter got the next two batters. Ortiz then singled to right and Ramirez hit a line drive homer to left to make it 3-2, Sox. Bradley then hit a grounder to third which Jake Lamb misplayed putting Bradley on. Holt singled and Holiday singled to drive Bradley in and it was 4-2.

In the last of the second, Pedroia and Bogaerts singled to start the inning. After Betts popped out, Ortiz singled to score Pedroia and Ramirez hit his second three run home in as many innings, deep to center, to make it 8-2. After scoring two runs in the first two innings, Pedroia left the game with flu like symptoms.

Tuffy Gosewisch got a lead off homer for Arizona in the fifth and

Ortiz got a lead off homer in the seventh to make it 9-3. The homer by Ortiz was his 1,000[th] extra base hit with the Sox, joining Ted Williams and Carl Yastrzemski as the only Sox players to reach that number.

Price lasted eight innings, leaving ahead 9-3, striking out eight and giving up 10 hits. Fernando Abad relieved Price in the ninth and, after getting the first two outs, gave up a double, single, walk and a run to make the final 9-4. Since coming over to the Sox from Minnesota, Abad had been in five games in relief, had given up four earned runs on six hits in just 3 2/3 innings and had lost two of the five games, not exactly an auspicious beginning for the 30 year old lefty.

Toronto was losing to the Yankees, 6-3, and Baltimore beat San Francisco 5-2 to move back into first place by ½ game over the Jays. The Sox gained a half game and were now 2 1/2 back of the Orioles but still only 3 ½ ahead of fourth place New York.

Clay Buchholz got his first start since July 2 in Game 2 and, as expected, didn't go deep into the game. He lasted 4 1/3 innings, giving up three runs in the fourth and fifth after shutting the Diamondbacks down for three innings and looking better than before he went to the bull pen. The Sox got one in the third on singles by Leon and Benintendi and an RBI single by Pedroia to go up 1-0.

Arizona scored in the fourth on a single by Bourn and a walk to Goldschmidt. They then pulled a double steal and Bourn scored when Lamb grounded into a force out. Weeks drove in Lamb with a single and it was 2-1. In the fourth, Owings singled and Buchholz got Hernandez to fly out for the first out. Ross relieved Buchholz and gave up a walk and a single scoring Owings to make it 3-1.

In the Boston fifth, Leon homered to lead off and Holt hit a fly to right which Brito let fall for an error and Holt ended up on second. Benintendi got his second hit, a double, driving in Holt, and Betts singled in Benintendi. In the sixth, Leon walked and Holt homered deep to right to make it 6-3.

After pitching a scoreless inning in the seventh, Barnes walked the first three batters in the eighth, loading the bases with no outs and the go ahead run at the plate. Ziegler came out of the bull pen and struck out the next three batters, on ten pitches, all strikes, to get out of the inning with no scoring and the final was 6-3. Kimbrel pitched a 1-2-3 ninth for his 19th save and Ross got the win, his second.

The last three batters in the lineup, Leon, Holt and Benintendi, scored all six Red Sox runs and had five hits in nine at bats between them. Benintendi now was 11-29, .379, in his first ten major league games and Leon raised his average to .390 with 48 hits in 123 at bats. Before this year, in four years of previous part time MLB experience, Leon had averaged .184 and had only 38 hits in 75 games, ten hits less that the 48 he had in 40 games this year.

Before the game, Manager Farrell presented Mookie Betts with the Major League Player of the Month Award for July. He had hit .368 with 15 RBI's and 5 homers in the month.

Baltimore lost to San Francisco, 6-2, and Toronto beat Houston, 4-2, to move back into first. Boston gained a half game and was two behind Toronto.

The Sox faced Zach Greinke, 11-3, in Game three and countered with Porcello, who was 15-3 and everyone expected a pitchers' duel. Boston surprised everybody, knocking Greinke out after just 1 2/3 innings, scoring nine runs on ten hits, to lead 9-0 after two innings.

A parade of six Arizona relievers could not stop the Sox as they scored 16 runs on 19 hits including three homers and a single by Mookie Betts, a homer by Bradley and five hits by Pedroia. Betts drove in eight runs, a career high and it was the fifth time Pedroia had had five hits in a game, the most times by any Red Sox player in history. Ramirez also had three hits as all nine starting players scored at least one run and only Holt, who played short for Bogaerts who is in a slump, went hitless. The final score was 16-2.

Betts now had 26 homers and 84 RBI's and raised his average to .313. He had three homers in one game on May 31 in Baltimore. Ted Williams was the only other Red Sox player to have hit three homers in a game twice in one season, accomplishing it in 1957.

Meanwhile, Porcello held the Diamondbacks to three hits and one run for seven innings, striking out four and walking no one, to make his record 16-3 and lower his ERA to 3.30.

Both Baltimore and Toronto won, so the standings remained the same, with the Sox two games out in third. They now left for an 11 game road trip starting with a single make up game in Cleveland on Monday. They then go to Baltimore for just two games and then on to Detroit for four and Tampa Bay for four before finally coming home. The 11 game trip includes 11 games in four different cities.

CHAPTER 17

THE SECOND LONG TRIP

AUGUST 15-25

The Sox started Drew Pomeranz, 8-9, against Josh Tomlin, 11-5, when they flew into Cleveland for the makeup game. After five innings, it was 1-0, Cleveland on a solo homer by Rajai Davis to lead off the Cleveland fourth. It stayed that way through five.

In the top of the sixth, Pedroia singled, his seventh hit in two games, and Ortiz hit his 27th homer to make it 2-1. With two out, Bradley homered to put the Sox up 3-1. It went to the last of the eighth with Pomeranz still on the mound and the score still 3-1. Giminez reached on a double and, with two out, Davis doubled to score him and put the tying run on second. Abad came in to pitch and got Ramirez to fly out to end the inning, 3-2, Boston.

In the top of the ninth, Hill singled and Shaw doubled to put men on second and third with no outs. McAllister who had come in to start the inning then got Holaday, Benintendi and Pedroia in order, to keep it at 3-2. Kimbrel came in in the last of the ninth to attempt to close the game for the Sox and gave up a double to Lindor and walked Napoli with no outs. He then struck out Santana and pinch hitter Kipnis and got Almonte to pop to second for the third out and the Sox had held on to win, 3-2.

Pomeranz went 7 2/3 innings, his longest stint in the majors, giving up just two runs on five hits to get the win and improving his record to 9-9. Kimbrel got his 20th save but was erratic again.

Ramirez is away on bereavement leave for three days. Steven Wright was placed on the fifteen day disabled list retroactive to August 8 which will make him eligible to come off the list before the end of the road trip.

After the game, the Sox traveled to Baltimore for a two game series in Camden Yard. They left Cleveland one game behind Baltimore and Toronto who were tied for first with an opportunity to pass the O's if they could take two in a row. Although slumping, the Orioles were still 39-17 at home.

In Game 1, on Tuesday night, Eduardo Rodriguez was on the mound for the Sox against Yovany Galliardo for the Orioles. The teams were scoreless for four innings with Rodriguez holding Baltimore hitless and striking out seven, including five of the last six he faced.

In the top of the fifth, Benintendi led off with a double to right and, after Pedroia grounded out, Bogaerts walked. Ortiz then struck out and Mookie Betts hit his 27th homer of the year to make it 3-0 Boston. In the last of the fifth, Rodriguez suffered tightness in his hamstring, later diagnosed as a cramp, and was replaced by Barnes, who pitched a scoreless fifth and sixth.

In the seventh, Barnes gave up a walk and a single with one out and was replaced by Abad who walked the first batter he faced to load the bases and gave up a two run single to Matt Wieters. Abad was replaced by Ziegler, who struck out J. J. Hardy before giving up a single to Kim to load the bases again. Ziegler then walked Jones to force in the tying run before striking out Schoop to get out of the inning with the score 3-3.

In the top of the eighth, Ortiz singled and Betts hit his second homer of the game to make it 5-3 going to the last of the eighth. Ziegler gave up a lead off single to Machado but then got a ground ball double play but hit the next batter and was relieved by Ross who struck out Hardy to end the inning.

It went to the last of the ninth, still 5-3 and Kimbrel came in in relief. Unlike most of his recent attempts at closing, there was no drama this time, as he got the Orioles in order for his 21st save. Ziegler got the win, his third and the win moved the Sox into a tie for second with Baltimore, one game behind the Blue Jays, who beat the Yankees 12-6 to take sole possession of first place. Betts drove in all five runs with two homers, giving him seven in Baltimore this year.

Game 2 started with David Price pitching for Boston against Dylan Bundy for Baltimore with a crowd of just 26,160 on hand. The Sox scored first in the top of the second when Bradley was hit by a pitch, moved to second on a single by Holt and scored on a single by Shaw. The Orioles came right back in their half of the inning with a solo homer by Chris Davis to make it 1-1.

In the third, with two outs, Betts walked and Bradley hit a long homer to center, his 20th, to make it 3-1. After Mookie Betts beat out a grounder to third and stole second in the fifth, Sandy Leon hit a massive homer to right that would have landed on Eutaw Street had it not hit a speaker on top of the fence, to make it 5-1.

In the sixth, Bogaerts singled to left and scored when Ortiz doubled to center. Betts then singled to right sending Ortiz to third and Bradley doubled to drive them both in and make it 8-1. As they started the seventh inning, the skies opened and, after a one hour and 18 minute rain delay, the game was called, giving the Red Sox the win.

Price went all the way, giving up the one run on just four hits, striking out four, walking none and lowering his ERA to 4.19 while improving his record to 11-8. Betts got two hits in three at bats and scored three runs. In the two game series, he went 4-7 with five RBI's and five runs scored.

The Sox had to fly to Detroit to start a four game series the next afternoon after the night game. By the time the Sox got to their hotel in Detroit to get ready for a one o'clock game it was 3:41 in the morning. Game 1 in Detroit would be Boston's fifth game in four different cities in the last five days. The good news was, as tired as they were getting into Detroit, they had won six in a row for the first time all year and were in second place alone, one game ahead of Baltimore and one behind first place Toronto, who beat the Yankees again, this time 7-4.

The Sox had tried to send starting pitcher Clay Buchholz to Detroit early to allow him to rest before his start in Game 1. However, he was unable to get out of Baltimore early and had to travel and pitch on short rest like the rest of the team.

He gave up a run in the second inning on a disputed play. J. D. Martinez led off with a single to left. Casey Mc Gehee then hit a liner to right which Bradley dove for and the umpire called it a catch, although it appeared that everybody in the ball park except the umpire had seen that it was a hit. Martinez retreated to first and Mc Gehee stayed on the bag while the ball came back in and Ramirez tagged them both. The replay showed the ball was a hit and the Tigers ended up with runners on first and third where they would have ended up if the original call had been correct.

Before play started again third base coach Brian Butterfield was ejected for objecting to the result of the replay. Jarrod Saltalamacchia then hit a sac fly to center and the Tigers were up 1-0. Leon led off the fourth for the Sox with his 7th homer and it was 1-1 after four. Buchholz lasted six innings, giving up the one run on six hits in his best performance of the year and left after six with the score still 1-1.

The Sox got two runs in the top of the eighth on successive singles by Bogaerts, Betts and Ramirez. Bogaerts scored on the hit by Ramirez and Betts scored on a wild pitch with two out and it was 3-1, Boston.

In the last of the eighth, Farrell brought in Tazawa to pitch even though Ziegler was available. Leading off the inning, Kinsler singled and Aybar doubled to put men on second and third with no outs. Cabrera then singled to center, driving in Kinsler and Farrell replaced Tazawa with Kinsler with men on first and second with no outs and Victor Martinez up. He singled to right to score Aybar and tie the game. J. D Martinez walked to load the bases and Ziegler got a force at the plate for the first out and struck out Saltalamacchia for the second. He then walked Romine, forcing in the go ahead run.

The Sox could not score in the ninth despite a walk to Holt and a single by Pedroia putting the tying run in scoring position with one out. Closer Francisco Rodriguez got Bogaerts to ground to first and got Betts on a hard liner right at the second baseman and the Sox had blown their first game in Detroit and broken their winning streak at six.

Tazawa got the loss for the Sox, giving up two singles and a double while getting no one out. In his last four appearances, he has given up seven hits and seven runs, while getting just six outs, in two innings of work. Farrell had the entire bull pen to pick from, except Ross who had pitched a perfect seventh, when he brought in Tazawa.

The Sox slipped to 1 ½ games behind idle Toronto with the loss, tied for second with the Orioles who beat Houston, 13-5.

After being held to three runs in Game 1, the day before, the Red Sox got four runs in the first inning on two run homers by Ortiz, his 28th of the year and 531st of his career, and Bradley, his 21st of the year, off Detroit starter Michael Fulmer, who came into the game 10-3. Porcello, who started for the Sox, gave up two in the second, one unearned. Pedroia made a throwing error on a ground ball to allow Victor Martinez to reach first leading off the second and J. D. Martinez then hit his 17th homer and it was 4-2.

The Sox got two in the Sixth when, with two outs, Leon and Holt singled. Benintendi singled to center to score Leon and Pedroia singled to right to score Benintendi, to make it 6-2. in the seventh, Ortiz and Betts singled to start the inning and Ramirez doubled to right to drive them both in and it was 8-2. In the top of the eighth, Benintendi led off with a double and Pedroia beat out a slow grounder to short. Ortiz was walked to load the bases and, with two out, Ramirez hit his second two run scoring double in as many innings and it was 10-2.

Hembree pitched a 1-2-3 eighth and Abad put the Tigers down in order in the ninth for a 10-2 Red Sox win. Porcello went seven innings, giving up just the two runs, only one earned, on three hits and striking out eight for his 17th win.   Ramirez had three hits and Pedroia, Bogaerts, Ortiz, Leon and Benintendi all had two hits each in the Boston 16 hit attack.

Toronto lost to Cleveland, 3-2, and the Orioles lost to Houston, 15-8, so the Sox moved to ½ game behind Toronto, in second place, one game ahead of Baltimore who slipped to third.

After a one hour and twenty minute rain delay, Drew Pomeranz, 9-9, started Game 3 against Detroit's Daniel Norris, 1-1. The Sox scored first in the third when Pedroia, Bogaerts and Ortiz loaded the bases with no outs on successive singles. Betts then grounded into a 6-4-3 double play and Pedroia scored to make it 1-0. In the bottom of the third, McCann led off with a homer to left for Detroit and it was 1-1.

In the fifth, Bogaerts led off with a double to left center and Ortiz followed with his 29th homer to make it 3-1, Boston. At the end of the fifth, the skies opened up and play was stopped.

After a one hour and eleven minute rain delay, play was resumed. Pomeranz, who had given up just the one run on only four hits, was replaced by Hembree, who got Kinsler, Aybar and Cabrera easily in the sixth. After getting one out in the seventh, he gave up a solo homer to J. D. Martinez to make it 3-2. Ziegler then relieved him and got the next two batters to end the inning.

Barnes took the mound for the Sox in the eighth and got two outs but walked two batters and was replaced by Kimbrel who got the last out. Kimbrel, despite giving up a double to the slumping Justin Upton, got through the ninth scoreless and got his 22d save as the Sox won 3-2. Pomeranz got his 10th win against nine losses and was very effective until the rain delay forced him out.

After Ortiz got his homer in the fifth, the next 18 Red Sox hitters were retired in order by the Tigers bullpen in relief of Norris. Bogaerts, whose average had slipped to .311 before the game, showed signs of coming out of the slump, getting two hits for the second game in a row.

The Sox stayed ½ game behind Toronto who edged Cleveland 6-5 and Baltimore fell to 2 ½ behind getting belted by Houston, 12-2. Baltimore had now lost six of their last ten, while the Sox were winning eight of ten.

Eduardo Rodriguez, scheduled to pitch the final game of the series after being out with what had been called a minor problem with a hamstring, notified Farrell the night before at around 5:30 p. m. that he would be unable to pitch the next day because it was still a problem.

Farrell contacted Pawtucket and had Henry Owens, who was supposed to pitch there in a couple of hours, scratched from the game there and come to Detroit to start the last game of the series. Owens, who had been getting ready to pitch in AAA, had to get to Detroit overnight and start a major league game at 1:00 the next afternoon against Justin Verlander.

Owens started and, in the first two innings, never gave up a batted ball in fair territory. He struck out five batters and walked two but one of those walked was thrown out stealing and, at the end of two it was 0-0.

In the third, he walked Saltalamacchia leading off, gave up a double to Aybar and, after getting two out, walked Cabrera intentionally to load the bases. J. D. Martinez then doubled to right to drive in two and Upton hit a 440 foot homer to left and it was 5-0. He got through the fourth with no scoring but, after Cabrera singled and Martinez doubled, with two out, in the fifth, Upton hit another tape measure, three run homer to left ending his personal hitting slump and making it 8-0.

In the sixth, Verlander gave up a lea doff triple to Benintendi, the first triple of his career. He scored on Pedroia's sac fly. Verlander left after six, ahead 8-1, having given up just three hits. In the last of the sixth, the Tigers added two more against Tazawa, who had replaced Owens, and it was 10-1.

In the last of the seventh, against Shane Greene, the Sox started with singles by Ramirez and Bradley. Another single by Leon scored Ramirez and Bradley scored when Shaw hit into a force out. Benintendi then hit the first homer of his career to score two more and it was 10-5 which was the final score.

Owens got his first loss of the year and continued to have the control problems that have haunted him the last three years. Tazawa had now given up two or more runs in four of his last five outings.

Fortunately for the Sox, Toronto lost to Cleveland 3-2 so they stayed one half game back, headed for a four game series in Tampa Bay against the last place Rays. The Orioles also lost to Houston 5-3 to remain 1 ½ games back of Boston.

David Price opened the series in Tampa Bay with a masterpiece against the admittedly weak hitting Rays. He went eight shutout innings and gave up just two hits while throwing 116 pitches and recording nine strikeouts to improve his record to 12-8 and his ERA to 4.00.

The Sox got two in the fourth off the Rays 23 year old, rookie starter, Blake Snell when Ramirez walked, Leon singled to right and Chris Young, in his first game back from this disabled list after a hamstring injury, doubled to left to score two. They added one in the seventh as Bogaerts scored on a sac fly by Ramirez to make it 3-0.

In the last of the eighth, with Beckham on first with only the Rays' second hit of the game, Steven Souza hit a drive into the left field corner just on the fair side of the foul pole. Benintendi got to the wall just as the ball was going over, leaped and caught the ball after it went over the wall and made perhaps the best catch of the baseball season to take away a homer and save two runs.

Benintendi, who had hit his first major league homer and triple the day before at Detroit, was hitting .306, with 19 hits and seven multiple hit games in his first 20 games since coming up on August 2. Not a bad start for a kid that was playing AA ball in Portland three weeks ago.

After Pedroia reached on a throwing error in the ninth, Bogaerts, who appeared to be out of his slump, hit his 15h homer to make it 5-0. Betts then singled, Ramirez doubled and Betts scored on a Leon ground out to make it 6-0.

Barnes came in to relieve Price in the ninth and gave up a two run homer to Evan Longoria to spoil the shutout but that was it as the Sox won, 6-2, to move into a tie with idle Toronto atop the American League East. Boston had not been in first since July 21. The Orioles beat Washington 4-3 and moved to two behind in third.

Game 2 was another thriller. The Sox, with Clay Buchholz on the mound again, led 2-0 after five after scoring two in the third on a single by Benintendi, who went to second on a grounder and scored on Ortiz' single to right. Ortiz then scored from first when Betts singled to right and Souza threw wild to third trying to get him.

Buchholz held the Rays to one run when Kiermaier doubled, with two outs, in the fifth to drive in Dickerson, who had singled. He left after 6 1/3, ahead 2-1.

After scoring in the third, the Sox bats died again and they managed just one single the rest of the way, Benintendi's second hit of the game, for a total of five hits against starter Chris Archer and four relievers. In the Rays' eighth, with one out Kiermaier doubled into the right field corner and tried to stretch it into a triple which would have put the tying run on third but Betts threw a strike to Shaw at third to cut him down and preserve the lead.

Ross relieved Buchholz in the seventh and got the two batters he faced to end that inning and Ziegler pitched a scoreless eighth, saved by Betts' throw. Kimbrel shut the Rays down in the ninth, despite hitting a batter with two outs, for his 23rd save.

Buchholz got his fifth win with his second consecutive quality start and now has an ERA of 3.00, in 27 innings, since being sent to the bullpen to work out his problems on July 21. Prior to that, his ERA was 5.91.

Both Baltimore and Toronto won so the Sox stayed tied with the Blue Jays in first.

Behind Rick Porcello, going after his 18th victory, the Sox got off to a quick start when Pedroia singled and stole second and Ortiz hit his 30th homer and drove in his 100th run of the season with a deep drive to right. It was his tenth year with 30 or more homers and 100 or more RBI's and the Sox were up 2-0. In the top of the third, Pedroia led off with a single, stole second again and scored on Betts' two out single to right to make it 3-0.

The Rays came back with two in the last of the second when Wilson and Kiermaier singled and Miller hit a double to right to score them both and make it 3-2. It stayed that way through six innings.

In the top of the seventh, Shaw beat out an infield grounder and Benintendi doubled to left to put men on second and third with no out. Pedroia then hit a chopper to short and Benintendi broke for third but Shaw stayed at third and, when Benintendi turned to go back to second, he twisted his knee and was tagged out by Duffy who then threw to first for the double play and the Sox did not score.

In the eighth, Porcello, despite having thrown 105 pitches stayed in. He got Kiermaier for the first out, the 11th consecutive batter he had retired. He then hung a curve to Evan Longoria who hit it for a homer and it was 3-3.

The Rays bullpen held the Sox at three runs, through the top of the eleventh. They hadn't scored after the third for the second night in a row. In the last of the eleventh, with two outs and Hembree pitching his second inning of relief, Wilson doubled and Forsythe hit a grounder that Shaw fielded at first and threw to Hembree covering. Hembree dropped the ball for an error and then threw home to try to stop Mikie Mahtook, who ran for Wilson, from scoring but Leon could not hold the throw and the run scored and gave the Rays the game 4-3.

The Blue Jays lost to the Angels, 8-2, and the Orioles beat Washington, 10-8, so the Jays and Sox remained tied for first with the O's now one game back.

For five innings of Game 4, starters Boston's Drew Pomeranz and Tampa's Jake Odorizzi locked in a scoreless duel. In the sixth, the Sox drew first blood when Holt and Pedroia singled and Bogaerts walked to load the bases. Betts then hit a sac fly to left to score Holt and, after Ramirez walked to reload the bases, Bradley hit into a 4-6-3 double play and the opportunity for a big inning went by the boards again.

In the last of the sixth, Longoria doubled and scored on a single by Miller and it was 1-1. Souza led off the Rays' seventh with a single to right and Mikie Mahtook, who scored the winning run the previous night, doubled to drive him in with what turned out to be the winning run as the Jays bullpen shut down the Sox the rest of the way again to win 2-1. In the last three games, against one of the weaker pitching staffs in baseball, the Sox had scored just six runs, scoring in only four innings, while being blanked in 25 innings.

Pomeranz had his best outing since joining the Sox, giving up just the two runs on seven hits and striking out a career high 11.

Toronto lost to the Angels, 6-3, and Baltimore was shut out by Washington, 4-0, behind a two hit, eight inning performance by Max Scherzer, leaving the Sox still tied for first with the Jays and the Orioles still one game back in third.

The Yankees, after having given up on the season and unloading many of their veterans at the trading deadline, remained 5 ½ games back at 65-61. The Eastern Division remained the only Division in baseball with four teams over .500 as, with just 35 games left, the young Sox continued to hold their own.

After the 11 game road trip, the Sox returned to Fenway to host the Kansas City Royals, one of the hottest pitching staffs in baseball, for a three game series.

The road trip, had consisted of 11 games, in four different cities, in 11 days, including four games in three different cities in the first four days, had been looked at as a possible disaster by Red Sox fans and the experts. The Sox left Fenway in third place, two games out of first, and had come home tied for first. A lot better result than most people had predicted.

CHAPTER 18

A SHORT VISIT HOME

AUGUST 26-31

The return to Fenway would be brief, only six games before hitting the road again to go out west, but after 11 games in four different cities, Boston must have looked good to the team.

Steven Wright, in his return from the disabled list, with his 13-5 record and 3.04 ERA took the mound for the Sox in Game 1 against the punchless Royals who had hit just 109 home runs and scored only 501 runs, 27th in the Major Leagues in both categories, coming into the game.

In the first inning of work since August 5th, Wright appeared to have no control of his knuckle ball at all, walked two batters and gave up five runs on a three run homer by Hosmer and a two run homer by Gordon. He the settled down and shut out the Royals for the next five innings, looking like the Steven Wright that had started the season.

Boston got one back in the first on singles by Pedroia, Bogaerts and Betts but, after loading the bases with one out, Royals' starter Ian Kennedy struck out Leon and Bradley and it was 5-1 after one inning. The Sox, who lately cannot hit with multiple runners on base, left eight men on base in the first four innings. They scored one more in the sixth when Holt doubled to right and Pedroia singled him in.

Cain had a lead off homer off Tazawa in the eighth to make it 6-2, Royals and it went to the last of the ninth that way. Pedroia and Bogaerts got back to back singles to lead off the ninth and the Royals brought in their Closer, Kelvin Herrera. Ortiz hit a liner up the middle which Herrera was able to knock down and threw to third to start an unusual 1-5-3 double play and there were two outs with a runner on second.

Betts then singled to right to drive in Bogaerts and make it 6-3 and Ramirez reached on a bloop single to right to bring the potential tying run to the plate with two outs. Leon then hit a soft grounder to second and the game was over.

The top four hitters in the Red Sox lineup had gone a collective 13-19, with Betts getting five hits, Pedroia four and Bogaerts three, but the rest of the lineup could manage just two hits as 12 runners were left on base. Betts raised his average to .324, Pedroia to .315 and Bogaerts, showing signs of coming out of his slump, to .308, while the fourth member of the top of the order Ortiz was at .320.

The Red Sox run in the ninth was the first run scored against the Royals' bullpen in 41 1/3 innings but it was too little too late as the Sox continued to be frustrated with multiple runners on base.

Toronto blasted Minnesota 15-8 dropping the Sox to second, one game back, while Baltimore lost again to the Yankees 14-4, staying in third, now two games out and just 3 ½ ahead of the Yankees.

In Game 2, the Sox got off to a 2-0 lead in the first, when Pedroia singled and Bogaerts hit a homer to left. The Royals came right back in the top of the second with back to back homers by Perez and Gordon off starter David Price. In the last of the second, Young walked, went to second on a passed ball and scored when Bradley hit a ground rule double to right. Pedroia then singled to drive in Bradley and it was 4-2, Red Sox.

In the fourth, Young walked again, went to second on a ground out and scored when Pedroia singled. It was Pedroia's tenth hit in a row over the last three games. They made it 7-2 in the fifth when Betts and Ramirez hit back to back homers. It was Betts' 29th and Ramirez' 17th. They added another in the sixth on a walk to Hill, Pedroia's eleventh hit in a row, a single, and a ground rule double by Bogaerts to make it 8-2.

After giving up the two runs in the first, Price held the Royals scoreless for the next five. Ziegler and Buchholz shut them out in the seventh and eighth and they got one run on Perez' second homer of the game to lead off the ninth against Ross who then shut them down for an 8-3 final.

Pedroia grounded into a double play to end the eighth and also end his hitting streak at 11 at bats, one short of the record of 12 held by three players, the Cubs Johnny Kling in 1902, the Red Sox Pinky Higgins in 1938 and the Tigers Walt Dropo, who also played for the Red Sox and was from Connecticut, in 1952.

Price got the win and improved his record to 13-8 and his ERA to 3.97. The Sox pounded Royals' starter Danny Duffy, who came into the game 11-1 for seven runs on eight hits in five innings.

The Blue Jays beat the Twins, 8-7, and the Orioles lost to the Yankees 13-5, so the Sox stayed one game behind Toronto and now led Baltimore by three.

The Sox went into Game 3 needing a win as Toronto and Baltimore had both won afternoon games. They started Eduardo Rodriguez, back from his hamstring problem. He gave up a homer to Perez, his third in two games, in the second. Gordon then singled to right and Escobar walked. Mondesi sacrificed them to second and third and Orlando hit a sac fly to center and it was 2-0, Royals.

The Sox came back with a homer by Ortiz, his 31st, in the fourth to make it 2-1. In the fifth, Young got an infield single, Leon hit a fly to center which was dropped by Orlando and there were runners on second and third with no out. Bradley walked to load the bases and Young scored when Holt grounded to first to make it 2-2. Bogaerts then singled to center to drive in two and it was 4-2.

In the sixth, after holding the Royals to two runs for five innings, Rodriguez walked Hosmer, gave up a ground rule double to

Morales and walked Perez to load the bases. Farrell brought in Barnes to relieve him and he gave up a single to Escobar on a slow roller to the mound, scoring Hosmer and leaving the bases loaded. Mondesi then tripled high off the center field wall to score three more. After Orlando was hit by a pitch, Cuthbert reached on a fielder's choice with Mondesi scoring and Cain singled to drive in another. Ross came in to relieve Barnes and gave up a single to Hosmer, scoring Cuthbert and Cain and making it 10-4 before he finally got out of the inning.

That was the final score as the Sox fell to two games behind Toronto. Rodriguez got his sixth loss with only two wins, giving up five runs, on four hits and four walks. Barnes gave up five runs on three hits and got no one out.

Tampa Bay, last in the American League East, was next in to Fenway for a three game series starting Monday night.

Rick Porcello started Game 1 and held the Rays to three runs on six hits, while striking out seven and walking no one for seven innings.

The Sox scored first in the second when Betts led off with his 30th homer high over the Green Monster. Ramirez then doubled, moved to third on a ground out and was thrown out at the plate when he tried to score on Young's grounder to Longoria at third. Leon then singled to left, Bradley walked and Holt singled to left scoring Young but Leon was thrown out at home trying to score from second by left fielder Dickerson to end the inning 2-0.

Porcello had his usual one bad inning in the third, giving up two runs on four consecutive singles and a sac fly to make it 2-2. Boston added three in the fourth on a single by Ramirez, consecutive doubles by Shaw and Young, and, after Leon and Bradley fanned, another double, this one by Holt and it was 5-2.

Dickerson doubled to lead off the fifth for the Rays, went to third on a ground out and scored on another grounder to make it 5-3.

Porcello got the next nine batters in order before leaving after seven.

The Sox got consecutive doubles, again, to lead off the fifth, this time by Ortiz and Betts with Ortiz scoring. Shaw then singled to score Betts and make it 7-3. They added two more in the last of the seventh when they loaded the bases on walks to Ramirez and Young and a single by Shaw. Leon then singled to drive in two and make it 9-3.

Buchholz pitched the eighth for Boston and gave up a run on two singles, a walk and a sac fly. Abad held the Rays scoreless in the ninth and the final was Boston 9 Tampa Bay 4.

Porcello got his league leading 18th victory. Holt, filling in for Pedroia, who was out for the second day due to a death in his family, and Shaw got three hits each in the 14 hit attack. They had six doubles to increase their league leading total to 290, 30 more than National League leader Colorado and 47 more than Houston the second highest in the American League.

The win kept them two games behind Toronto but now two ahead of third place Baltimore and, perhaps more importantly, in first place in the race for the two Wild Card positions.

The Sox started Drew Pomeranz in Game 2 against Jake Odorizzi for the Rays. The Rays scored in the first on a double by Kiermaier who scored on a single by Miller. The Sox tied it in the fifth on a homer by Ramirez, his 18[th,] and got two more in the sixth on a walk to Pedroia, a double by Bogaerts, a sac fly by Ortiz and a run scoring single by Ramirez, to make it 3-1.

Pomeranz gave up a lead off single to Beckham in the seventh and, with two out, Maile homered to tie the game at 3-3.

Buchholz came on in the eighth and gave up a one out homer to Longoria and that was all the scoring as the Rays won 4-3. Boston had two runners on in the ninth on a single by Ramirez, his third hit of the game, and a walk to Young but Leon, hitting for Holaday, took three called strikes to end the game.

Pomeranz looked good for 6 2/3 innings despite giving up the homer in the seventh, striking out eight and giving up just three hits. Buchholz took the loss, his tenth.

Baltimore beat Toronto, 5-3, so the Sox stayed two games back but now were only one ahead of the third place Birds.

In the final game of the home stand, the Rays started Drew Smyly against David Wright. Wright got off to a shaky start again, giving up a run in the first on a single by Kiermaier and a double by Miller. In the second, he gave up two more when Wilson doubled and Forsythe homered. The Sox had gotten a run in the last of the first on Bogaerts' 17th homer of the year and it was 3-1 after three innings.

In the fourth, Morrison homered to lead off the Rays' half of the inning. Beckham followed with a single and Forsythe walked. Kiermaier singled and was thrown out trying to stretch it into a double, by Betts. In a rare happening, Beckham slowed down before crossing home and had not touched home when Kiermaier was thrown out at second so Beckham's run did not count and it was 4-1 after four.

Bradley and Pedroia led off the sixth with singles and, after two were out, Betts walked to load the bases. Hanley Ramirez then hit a grand slam homer and the Sox were up 5-4. They added another run in the last of the seventh when Bradley homered to left and it was 6-4.

Abad, the third reliever for the Sox, loaded the bases on two singles and a walk in the eighth and was replaced by Tazawa in his first outing since returning. He immediately gave up a two run scoring single to Forsythe and the game was tied, 6-6.

The Sox came back in the last of the eighth when Ramirez drew a lead off walk, was sacrificed to second by Leon and went to third on a single by Holt, hitting for Young. Hill then singled to right to score him and Bradley doubled to right to score Holt and the Sox were ahead by two again, 8-6.

Kimbrel got the Rays 1-2-3 in the ninth for his 24th save and Tazawa, despite the fact that he only got one out and gave up a two run scoring single, got the win to improve his record to 3-2. Wright lasted just four innings, giving up five runs on seven hits and three walks.

Pedroia had three hits in five at bats and was now 17 for his last 25 and had raised his batting average to .323, second best in the league, ahead of Betts, in third at .320, Ortiz, seventh at .313 and Bogaerts tenth at .306.

Toronto beat Baltimore, 5-3, so the Sox stayed two back while the Orioles fell to four games out, two behind the Sox. The Yankees beat the Royals, 5-4, and now trailed Baltimore by just 2 ½ games.

Yoan Moncada was added to the roster as the Sox left for the road trip. Moncada, a switch hitting infielder, is expected to platoon at third base where the Sox had been getting no production from Shaw and Hill. Although the switch hitting 21 year old had never played higher than AA ball, he was the highest rated player in the Sox minor league system, hitting .294 with 15 homers and 45 stolen bases between A and AA ball this year. He was also the MVP in the Futures Game played in July.

The Sox now traveled west for a three game series with Oakland and another with San Diego before heading back to Toronto for a three game series that could be the biggest of the year.

CHAPTER 19

ON THE ROAD AGAIN

SEPTEMBER 1-11

They started David Price against the Athletics in Game 1 and he responded with seven innings of four hit ball, giving up just two runs while the Sox were pounding Oakland pitching for a total of 17 hits and 16 runs. Price left after seven, ahead 12-2, and Joe Kelly and Robby Scott, both just up from Pawtucket, pitched scoreless innings in the eighth and ninth as the Sox won 16-2.

Shaw started at third and went 3-6 with two doubles and a three run homer, driving in five and scoring two. The Sox scored in six different innings, with four in the fifth and six in the sixth. In addition to Shaw's performance, Pedroia, Ortiz, Ramirez and Leon all had two hits apiece in the rout. Moncada got into his first game in the seventh, replacing Ramirez but playing third as Shaw moved to first. His first time up in the eighth, he walked and scored a run and then struck out swinging in the ninth.

Price improved his record to 14-8 and his ERA to 3.92. He has now won his last five starts, pitching 35 innings with a 2.06 ERA, 34 strikeouts and just eight walks.

Toronto lost to Tampa Bay, 8-3, moving the Sox to one game behind the Jays, and Baltimore shut out the Yankees 8-0 to stay two behind Boston.

The following article appeared on my blog baseballworldbjt.com on September 3, 2016.

SOX STRENGTHEN BULLPEN, FINALLY

It's that time of the year, the rosters are expanded and dugouts and bullpens will be full of players from now until the Playoffs when everyone will scramble to decide who stays on the 25 man roster for the second season. The Red Sox, in the thick of things, now just one game out of first, made some moves of their own.

In addition to Yoan Moncada, the 21 year old, switch hitting, highly touted infielder they activated from AA Portland to give them some production at third base, they added several other players as the rosters expanded.

They reactivated catcher Ryan Hanigan from the disabled list and brought up Deven Marrero, a utility infielder from Pawtucket who has done time in Boston earlier this year.

In a move to strengthen their bullpen, where someone said this week 'leads go to die', they also brought up Robby Scott, a left handed pitcher, from Pawtucket, where he had a 2.54 ERA in 32 games there, including 6 starts and 26 relief appearances. This is the same Robby Scott who pitched the ninth inning last night and, in his first big league appearance, struck out two batters and held the Athletics scoreless.

And, oh yes, they also recalled Joe Kelly from Pawtucket. In his last 13 relief appearances in Pawtucket, he had a 0.56 earned run average and struck out 25 batters while only walking two.

This is the same Joe Kelly that started and won eight games in a row from August 1st until September 9th last year, while posting a 2.59 earned run average with just 14 earned runs in 48 2/3 innings. This is the same Joe Kelly that averages 95.3 miles per hour on his four seam fastball and who came out of the bullpen last night and struck out two Oakland batters in the eighth inning while holding them scoreless.

Maybe I'm missing something, so tell me again why Farrell had to go to Fernando Abad and Junichi Tazawa in the 7th and 8th on Wednesday afternoon or to Clay Buchholz in the 8th on Tuesday night and to Buchholz and Abad in the 8th and 9th on Monday and why the bullpen had nobody left in it, except Buchholz, when Kimbrel came in to save the game on Wednesday.

CARL H. JOHNSON,
September 3, 2016

In Game 2, Boston continued to pummel Oakland pitching, scoring 11 runs on 17 hits, to bring the total runs scored in five games against them this year to 67, while winning 11-2.

Porcello, who had a perfect game going for 5 1/3 innings before giving up a double in the sixth, went seven innings for his 19th win, the highest total in the majors. He gave up just two runs on four hits and walked none while lowering his ERA to 3.23. Abad and Tazawa were able to get through the eighth and ninth with no scoring.

The Sox started out with two in the first on another lead off single by Pedroia, a double by Ortiz and a two run double by Betts, bringing his RBI total to 100. After two were out and no one on, they scored seven in the third, started by Ramirez's 20th homer. They sent nine batters to the plate after two were out and had seven hits. including three doubles, one Moncada's first big league hit, driving in two runs.

The game was effectively over at that point although the Athletics scored single runs in the sixth and seventh and the Sox added one each in the eighth and ninth. Boston emptied the bench, using 15 position players in the game. Ortiz had three hits and Pedroia, Bogaerts, Leon, Moncada and Bradley all had two

Toronto lost to Tampa again, this time 7-5, moving the Sox into a tie for first, and Baltimore kept pace, shutting out the Yankees again, this time 2-0.

After scoring 67 runs in the first five games of the season against Oakland, the Sox were shut out by three Oakland pitchers in Game 3 and lost 1-0. Eduardo Rodriguez pitched a no hitter for 7 2/3 innings until Oakland's Marcus Semien hit a ground ball that hit Rodriguez in the foot and bounced away. Rodriguez picked it up and threw to first and the umpire called Semien out. The Athletics appealed and the call was overturned on replay and

Oakland had their first hit. Rodriguez got the third out on a come backer and the game went to the ninth 0-0.

The Sox had had the bases loaded in the fourth with one out and couldn't score. They also had runners on first and second in the seventh and couldn't score. The Sox could manage just six hits, all singles, including two hits each by Pedroia and Moncada.

The game went to the ninth, still 0-0. Ryan Madson, the Athletics Closer got the Sox 1-2-3 in the top half. Kimbrel came on in the last of the ninth for the Sox. He walked Danny Valencia on five pitches and Khris Davis hit a ball off the left field wall that took a bad hop on Holt and he couldn't field it cleanly, allowing Valencia to score from first and the Athletics had won 1-0.

Kimbrel got the loss and Madson the win while Rodriguez, who gave up just the one infield hit in eight innings, got no decision in what was probably the best performance of his career.

Toronto beat the Rays 5-3, dropping the Sox into second, one game back. Baltimore lost to the Yankees, 5-2, to stay two behind the Sox.

The Sox opened their three game series in San Diego on Labor Day. After being shut out the day before by the Athletics, the Red Sox were held scoreless for seven innings of Game 1 by 32 year old, right hander Edwin Jackson, who came into the game with a 3-5 record and a 6.26 ERA and struck out 11 while allowing just four hits.

Pomeranz started for the Sox and gave up just two runs on six hits in 5 2/3 innings. The two runs came in the fourth when Dickerson walked and Adam Rosales, a .222 hitter, batting seventh, homered over the left field wall. The Sox only run came in the eighth when Young, hitting for Holaday, leading off the inning, hit the first pitch of reliever Brad Hand for a homer.

Hill, hitting for Holaday, then doubled and moved to third on a ground out by Pedroia. Leon, hitting for Holt, then struck out and the pitch bounced away from the catcher and Hill came home with what looked like the tying run. The third strike had hit Leon on the foot after he swung at it so Hill was sent back to third and Bogaerts struck out to end the threat.

Ramirez got an infield single, his third hit of the game, with one out in the ninth but was left stranded and the Sox lost 2-1. In the last 18 innings, against two of the weaker teams in baseball, the Sox had scored just one run on 13 hits and struck out 23 times.

Pomeranz, who didn't pitch badly got the loss. Hembree, Ross and Kelly pitched scoreless ball after Pomeranz left. Kelly had a 1-2-3 eighth with two strikeouts, throwing 100 miles an hour with great control.

The Yankees beat the Jays so the Sox stayed one back but the Orioles beat the Rays to gain a game and were now one back of the Sox.

Before the start of Game 2 in San Diego, the Sox knew that Toronto had lost to the Yankees, 7-6, and that they could move back into a tie for first with a win.

With David Wright still having trouble with his shoulder, Buchholz started for the Sox. Paul Clemens was on the hill for the Padres and it was scoreless after three. In the fourth. Leon bunted to third with the shift on and only the short stop on that side and reached for a single. Bradley then hit his 23rd homer to right and Young followed, back to back, with his second homer in two nights and 8th of the year to make it 3-0.

The Padres got a lead off homer from Ryan Schimpf to start the bottom half of the fourth to make it 3-1 but the Sox came back in the top of the fifth on singles by Bogaerts and Betts and another by Ramirez, scoring Bogaerts. After Bradley was walked intentionally to load the bases, Young hit a grounder to third forcing Bradley at second but scoring Betts with the final run of the game, making it 5-1.

Buchholz went 6 2/3 innings, giving up just the one run on eight hits and, more importantly, walking none and striking out six. Barnes got the last out in the seventh and Abad pitched a 1-2-3 eighth. Kelly pitched another scoreless inning in the ninth despite giving up a lead off single. Buchholz was now 6-10 and lowered his ERA to 4.99, the first time this year that his ERA had been under 5.00.

The Sox had 10 hits, including two each by Pedroia, Betts and Young. Pedroia raised his average to .325, second best in the American League and he now had 25 hits in his last 47 at bats in 11 games, a .532 average. He trails Houston's diminutive second baseman, Jose Altuve, by 19 points for the lead. Yoan Moncada, struggling since going 2-4 in the finale at Oakland, struck out four times in four at bats, giving him seven consecutive strikeouts and 10 in 17 at bats since joining the Sox.

Baltimore beat Tampa Bay 11-2 to move to one game behind Toronto and Boston who were tied in first again.

In Game 3 at San Diego, David Price went seven innings, giving up just two runs on six hits while striking out eight and walking none. He gave up a run in the first when Myers singled and scored on Solarte's double to left and another in the third when Myers hit a sac fly to left with the bases loaded.

The Sox had gotten two in the second when Shaw hit a two out homer to right, his 16th, driving in Bradley who had walked. They got three more in the fourth when Bradley reached on an error at first by Myers, Young singled and Shaw singled driving in Bradley. Young and Shaw then pulled a double steal and Pedroia doubled to left to drive them both in, making it 5-2.

Ramirez hit his 21st homer to lead off the eighth and Holt got his 7th in the ninth to make the final, 7-2. Uehara, just off the disabled list, pitched a 1-2-3 eighth, striking out two. Ziegler started the ninth and had two outs with a runner on first when Kimbrel relieved him and got the last out.

The win made Price 15-8 on the season and lowered his ERA to 3.87.

Toronto was shut out by the Yankees, 2-0, sweeping their series, and Baltimore lost to the Rays, 7-6, leaving the Sox alone in first place, one ahead of Toronto and two ahead of Baltimore, headed to Toronto for a three game series after a day off on Thursday.

With 23 games remaining, all against Eastern Division teams, the Sox were 17 games over .500 with a record of 78-61. The 78 wins matched their total for all of 2015.

The following article appeared in my blog on September 9. 2016.

THE REAL RACE BEGINS

The Boston Red Sox and Toronto Blue Jays meet tonight in the first of a three game series in the Rogers Center in Toronto. The Sox go into the series in first place, one game ahead of the Blue Jays and two ahead of the Baltimore Orioles in the American League East.

If the season ended today, all three of those teams would be in the playoffs, the Red Sox as the Division Winner and the other two as the American League Wild Cards. However, there are still 23 games for each team to play before the regular season is over.

Looking at the schedule, it appears that the Red Sox have the tougher schedule of the three the rest of the way. The Sox play all 23 of their games against Eastern Division opponents while the Jays have seven games outside the division and the Orioles have six.

So far this season the Red Sox have fared the worst against Eastern Division opponents, winning 28 and losing 25, while the Jays are 32-28 and the O's 32-27. The Eastern Division, the strongest division for a long time, had faded over the last few years.

Last year, at this time, the Eastern Division only had two teams over .500 and, this year, it is the only division in baseball with four teams over .500. Even the fourth place Yankees are only two games out of a wild card spot at this time.

The Eastern Division, with a record of 364 wins and 331 losses has the highest winning percentage of any of the six divisions. Their winning percentage is 19 points higher than the second highest division, the National League Central. These numbers include all games, including inter-league play. By the way, for what it's worth, the American League has won 157 and lost just

123 to National League teams this year.

The Sox have a rough road ahead. Their starting pitching appears to have peaked going into the stretch. They have Uehara back in the bull pen and Kelly appears to be over his problems giving them another arm there. They have certainly demonstrated an ability to put enough runs on the board.

It's going to be a tough battle, but don't count them out, this is a young team with unlimited potential. We are getting closer to a Fenway Park and Wrigley Field World Series every day.

CARL H. JOHNSON
September 9, 2016

With Marco Estrada, who had beaten them twice earlier in the season, on the mound for Toronto, the Sox sent Rick Porcello, 19-3 after his 20th victory in Game 1.

The Sox jumped on Estrada for one in the first on a lead off single by Pedroia and a run scoring double by Betts. After Ramirez and Shaw walked to load the bases, Leon grounded out and they had to settle for one run. They got another in the second when Bradley walked, went to second on a wild pitch and scored on Pedroia's second hit in two innings, making it 2-0.

They added two in the the third on singles by Betts and Ramirez, a sac fly by Shaw and a run scoring single by Leon, to go up 4-0. Toronto came back in their half of the third when they loaded the bases with no outs on a walk and two singles and a single by Travis drove in two to make it 4-2.

Holt led off the fourth with a double, went to third on a passed ball and scored when Pedroia hit a sac fly to center and it was 5-2, Sox. It stayed that way until the top of the seventh when the Sox got six runs on six hits, including a solo homer by Bogaerts to lead off the inning, a double by Ortiz and a three run homer by Ramirez, another double by Bradley and a two run scoring single by Pedroia and it was 11-2.

Toronto got another in the eighth and the Sox added two more in the ninth for a 13-3 final.

Porcello, as usual, had the one bad inning, but went seven, giving up just two runs on six hits and striking out seven for his 20th win, lowering his ERA to 3.21. Ziegler pitched the eighth, giving up an unearned run and Uehara pitched the ninth, giving up a single but getting two strikeouts and looking like the Uehara of old.

The Sox had 18 hits. Pedroia had three and Bogaerts, Ortiz, Betts, Ramirez, Leon and Bradley all had two each.

Boston was now in first, two ahead of Toronto, three up on third place Baltimore, who lost to Detroit, 4-3, and four up on the Yankees, who moved to one behind Baltimore in fourth place with a 7-5 win over Tampa Bay.

After scoring 13 runs on 18 hits in Game 1, the Sox were no hit for 4 1/3 innings in Game 2 by Toronto starter J. A. Happ. The Jays got on the board in the second when Melvin Upton hit a homer with Martin aboard to make it 2-0. They got another in the third after Hill, playing third, booted Encarnacion's grounder to put runners on first and third with one out. Bautista then hit a little blooper into left which fell, driving in Donaldson with the third run, this one unearned.

Young singled in the fifth to break up the no hitter but the Sox could not score. Pedroia led off the sixth with his 13th homer, making it 3-1.

In the seventh, Ramirez and Hill hit back to back singles to start the inning and Toronto brought in right hander Joaquim Benoit in relief. With left handed batters Leon, Holt and Shaw available, Farrell let right handed batter Young hit for himself and he hit a foul pop to short right for the first out. Bradley then hit a long drive which Bautista caught at the base of the wall in right to score Hill but Shaw, batting for Hanigan, struck out to end the inning and it was 3-2.

Grilli pitched a scoreless eighth for Toronto and Closer Osuna held the Sox in the ninth for his 31st save and a 3-2 win for Toronto. Farrell let Young hit for himself in the ninth, against the right handed Osuna, with one out and a runner on first and he fouled out to the catcher.

Rodriguez had a good outing, giving up just two earned runs on four hits in seven innings but Hill's error cost him the loss as he fell to 2-7. Barnes, despite giving up two singles pitched a scoreless seventh and Kelly, looking sharp again with a fast ball at 100 miles an hour, struck out two and walked one in a scoreless eighth.

The win moved Toronto to one game behind Boston again with the third game of the series coming up on Sunday.

The Red Sox started Clay Buchholz in Game 3 against Toronto's Aaron Sanchez. In one of the wildest games of the year, the Sox and Rays used nine pitchers each, each team had three homers, Boston pitching struck out 13 Jays and walked seven and Jays pitching struck out 11 Sox and walked six, the Red Sox scored in six of the first seven innings and the Jays in three of the first four and an attempted steal of home to try to tie the score in the fifth was unsuccessful.

The Sox got one in the first to go ahead and added three in the second on Bradley's 24th homer. The Jays had gotten one back in the last of the first on Encarnacion's first of two homers and it was 4-1 after two. The Jays got five in the third, including a grand slam homer by Tulowitzki and it was 6-4 Jays.

The Sox came back with two in the top of the fourth when Bogaerts singled to drive in Bradley, who had singled and Pedroia, who had doubled, and it was tied at 6-6. In the last of the fourth, Hembree replaced Buchholz and Encarnacion hit his second homer with Donaldson on and it was 8-6.

In the fifth, with one out, Ramirez hit a solo homer 444 feet to straight away center to make it 8-7. With two outs, Holt was on third and tried to steal home but was thrown out. In the sixth after Pedroia and Bogaerts singled with one out, Ortiz hit a three run homer, his 32nd, and it was 10-8. It was his 535th homer and put him one ahead of Jimmy Foxx and one behind Mickey Mantle. The Sox added another in the seventh on a walk to Holt and a double by Leon to make it 11-8.

After Hembree gave up the homer in the fourth, seven relievers held the Jays scoreless for the rest of the game and the final was 11-8.

Kimbrel, though wild, pitched a scoreless ninth for his 25th save. With a runner on first and one out in the ninth, Martin hit a fly into the right field corner for an apparent double, bringing the tying run to the plate. The Red Sox objected to the call and the umpires, after conferring, called the ball foul. Toronto challenged the call and, after the replay, the foul call was confirmed and Martin then struck out for the second out of the inning. Kimbrel then got Tulowitzki to fly out to Betts in deep right and the game was over.

Pedroia had two hits to make him 16 for 38 on the road trip and Bogaerts and Bradley had two hits each as the Red Sox got their 11 runs on just 11 hits.

The win made the Sox 6-3 on the road trip and put them two games up on Toronto and Baltimore, who were tied for second. At the start of the nine game trip, they had been two games behind Toronto in second place.

They now headed for Fenway to play three games with Baltimore followed by a four game set with the Yankees.

CHAPTER 20

BACK HOME AGAIN

SEPTEMBER 12-18

In Game 1 against Baltimore, in Friendly Fenway, David Price started against former Red Sox pitcher Wade Miley. After Price set the Orioles down 1-2-3 in the first, the Sox loaded the bases in the bottom half on singles by Pedroia, Bogaerts and Ortiz with no outs. Betts then doubled off the left field wall to score two. Ramirez then singled to score Ortiz and, when Baltimore left fielder, Steve Pearce, lobbed the ball back into the infield Betts kept running around third and scored the fourth run. After Young singled, Leon hit a sac fly to center to score the fifth run and it was 5-0 Red Sox and the game was effectively over.

The Sox got single runs in the second, when Worley, in relief of Miley, walked in a run; in the third when Young doubled, Leon singled and Bradley hit a sac fly; in the fourth on a solo homer by Ramirez; in the fifth on a solo homer by Young and in the sixth on a solo homer by Ortiz. They got two more in the seventh on a single by Hill, a double by Young, and a single by Leon. Young then scored on a ground out by Bogaerts to make it 12-2 and the Red Sox had scored in seven innings in a row.

In the meantime, Price was giving up just two runs on solo homers by Davis and Machado and no other hits in eight innings to make the final 12-2.

Price got his 16th win with 8 losses and lowered his ERA to 3.81. Ortiz's homer was his 33rd of the year and put him in 17th place overall, tied with Mickey Mantle. Ramirez's was his 24th and Young's his 9th. Young had three other hits in the game including two doubles. Pedroia had two hits in four at bats to raise average to .330, still second in the league.

The Blue Jays beat Tampa Bay, 3-2, to stay one game back and

Baltimore fell to three behind. The Yankees lost to the Dodgers and fell five back.

Drew Pomeranz started Game 2 for the Red Sox and gave up a single to Trumbo, a walk to Davis and a three run homer by Hardy to begin the second. He then walked Stubbs and the number nine hitter, Reimold, who had victimized the Sox on the last day in 2011, homered to make it 5-0. Pomeranz struck out the next two batters but gave up a lead off single to Machado and was then removed and Heath Hembree replaced him.

The Sox had loaded the bases in their half of the second on a double by Shaw, a walk to Young and a single by Bradley. The O's starter Dylan Bundy, then walked Hanigan and Pedroia to force in two runs but Bogaerts struck out and Ortiz grounded out to end the inning with the score, 5-2, Baltimore.

Bogaerts led off the fifth with a homer to left, his 19th, to make it 5-3 and that was all the scoring for Boston. Farrell used six relievers and they held the O's scoreless until the top of the ninth, when Noe Ramirez, gave up a solo homer to Schoop and the final was 6-3, Baltimore. Zach Britton had come with two out in the eighth for Baltimore and got a four out save, his 42nd of the year.

Andrew Benintendi was reactivated from the disabled list for the Sox before the game but did not play.

Bundy lasted 5 1/3 innings and got his ninth win. Pomeranz, who only got four outs, while giving up five runs on four hits and two walks, got the loss to make him 10-12 on the year and 2-5 with a 4.60 ERA, in 11 starts, since joining the Sox.

Tampa Bay beat Toronto 6-2 to keep the Sox two games up on the Jays but Baltimore moved into a tie for second, two back. The Yankees shut out the Dodgers, 3-0, with all their runs coming on homers, to get back to four games out.

Toronto lost an afternoon game the next day to Tampa Bay 8-1 so the Red Sox went into Game 2 against Baltimore at night with the chance to go three up on both the Jays and O's.

With 20-3 Rick Porcello, who hadn't lost a game in 13 decisions at Fenway, against Baltimore's Kevin Gausman, 7-10, the Sox looked to have a good chance to up the lead.

In the top of the second, Mark Trumbo led off with his 42nd homer to put Baltimore up 1-0 and that was it. Gausman held the Sox scoreless for eight on just four hits while Porcello went eight and gave up just the one run. Britton pitched the ninth for the O's and got Ortiz, Betts and Ramirez in order for his 43rd save.

Porcello suffered his first Fenway loss of the season after the being the first Red Sox pitcher to go 13-0 at home at the start of the season since Dave Ferris in 1946. His first loss at home made him 20-4 overall with a 3.12 ERA.

The win moved Baltimore into second place alone, one game behind Boston and left Toronto two back in third and the Yankees, who lost to the Dodgers, 2-0, four games behind. The Yankees were coming in Thursday night to open a four game series.

Down 5-1 going to the last of the eighth in Game 1, the Sox engineered one of the most dramatic finishes in baseball this year to win 7-5 in Game 1 against the Yankees.

In the last of the eighth, trailing 5-1, Ortiz hit his 34th homer of the year deep over the center field wall to make it 5-2. Betts followed with an infield single and, with two outs, Shaw walked to put the tying run at the plate in the person of Sandy Leon. Leon struck out and the rally was over.

After Joe Kelly loaded the bases with Yankees in the top of the ninth on two singles and a walk with just one out, he struck out Chase Headley and got Rob Refsnyder to line back to him for the third out and the game went to the last of the ninth with the Yankees still up, 5-2.

With one out in the last of the ninth and Young, who had been hit by a pitch and Pedroia, who had walked, on base, they moved to second and third on defensive indifference. Bogaerts then hit a tapper to the right of the mound which Yankee Closer Dellin Betances fielded and threw home to get Young for the second out.

Ortiz then hit a 3-1 pitch on a line to center for a single to score Pedroia and move Bogaerts to third. Hernandez was sent in to run for Ortiz and Betts hit a ground shot between third and short for a single, scoring Bogaerts.

With two outs and the score 5-4, Yankee catcher Sanchez let a pitch get by him and the runners moved to second and third. Hanley Ramirez came up as the potential winning run. With the count 3 and 1, he hit a Betances 99 mile an hour fast ball 426 feet to the center field seats and the Red Sox had come from behind to win, 7-5.

Fenway Park went wild as Ramirez crossed the plate and the players celebrated on the field. The Orioles had lost to Tampa Bay, 7-6, so the Sox were back to two games ahead of Baltimore and Toronto beat the Angels 7-2 to stay two back.

Hanley's dramatic homer was his 25th of the year and gave him 100 RBI's. Ortiz had three hits and drove in three runs and Benintendi, back in left after being on the disabled list, was 1-3 with a double. Kelly got the win in relief to improve his record to 3-0.

Eduardo Rodriguez started for the Sox but gave up five runs in 2 1/3 innings before being replaced by Hembree who went 1 2/3 before Tazawa pitched a scoreless fifth, striking out the side after giving up a lead off double.

Twenty seven year old, Robby Scott, in just his second big league game for Boston, held the Yankees scoreless in the sixth, seventh and eighth.

After their dramatic, come from behind win, in Game 1, Boston got off to a quick start in Game 2, scoring two in the first. Pedroia singled to left and was thrown out at second trying to stretch it into a double. Bogaerts was then hit with a pitch and went to second on a wild pitch. Ortiz then singled to drive him in but was thrown out at second trying to stretch the single into a double.

Betts then singled to left and was called out at second trying to steal. The Sox appealed the call and he was ruled safe, avoiding three runners being thrown out at second in one inning. Ramirez then singled to score Betts to make it 2-0.

Ramirez hit his 26th homer of the season in the fourth, to make it 3-0. Since August 1, in 38 games, Ramirez had now driven in 40 runs.

The Yankees got two in the fifth on singles by Teixeira and Williams and a two run double by Rookie catcher Gary Sanchez to make it 3-2.

The Sox got two more in the sixth when they loaded the bases on a double by Ortiz, a single by Betts and a walk to Ramirez. Shaw hit a sac fly to score Ortiz and Leon doubled to score Betts. In the seventh, Bradley hit a lead off homer, his 25th. Pedroia then singled and scored on Bogaerts doubled off the left field wall and it was 7-2.

Buchholz, who had started for the Sox, left after five having given up just two runs. Ross, Ziegler and Uehara held the Yankees scoreless through the eighth. In the ninth, Abad came on and gave up a two run homer to Billy Butler, just acquired by the Yankees from Oakland, hit another batter and was relieved by Kimbrel, who struck out the next two batters for a 7-4 win and his 26th save. Buchholz got the win and made his record 7-10.

Baltimore beat Tampa Bay and the Blue Jays beat the Angels so the standings stayed the same, except that the Yankees fell to six games back and four out of the Wild Card race.

The Yankees got off to a quick start in Game 3 against David Price, scoring three in the third on a single by Romine, who scored when Gardner tripled to deep center. Gary Sanchez then homered to make it 3-0, Yankees. It was his 15th homer in his first 40 games in the big leagues.

The Sox came back with two in the bottom half of the third on doubles by Benintendi and Bogaerts. Bogaerts then went to third on a passed ball and scored when Ortiz grounded out to second, making it 3-2.

In the fourth, Gregorius and Headley singled and Romine doubled to deep left, scoring them both and making it 5-2, New York. In the Red Sox fifth, Bradley walked and, with two out, Bogaerts hit his 20th homer to make it 5-4. Bogaerts became the fourth Red Sox player to hit 20 or more this year.

Price left after six, behind 5-4, having given up nine hits and striking out seven. Ross relieved Price and got just one out before being replaced by Barnes who got through the seventh with no scoring.

In the Boston seventh, Bogaerts doubled and Betts singled to drive him in to tie the score. Ramirez then singled and Shaw grounded out to first with Betts and Ramirez moving to second and third. Betts scored on a wild pitch and Ramirez was out at the plate trying to score on the same play but the Sox were up 6-5 .

In the eighth, with two outs, Barnes walked Gregorius and Kimbrel replaced Barnes. He struck out Headley to end the inning and then struck out Romine, Williams and Gardner in order in the ninth for his 27th save. It was the first time in his career that Kimbrel got a four out save with all four outs strikeouts. Bogaerts had two doubles and a homer for the Sox and Ramirez got three hits, including a double, raising his average to .290. Barnes got the win bringing his record to 4-3.

The Orioles lost to Tampa Bay, 5-2, and the Blue Jays were beaten

6-1 by the Angels so the Red Sox gained a game on both teams and were up three games on each with the Yankees now seven games back and four out of the Wild Card race.

In the finale against the Yankees, on Sunday night, Pomeranz started for the Sox against the Yankee C. C. Sabathia. Pomeranz had control problems from the beginning. He gave up a lead off double to Gardner in the first, walked Butler and Gregorius then singled to drive in Gardner to make it 1-0.

Gary Sanchez hit a solo homer in the third and Butler and Gregorius followed with singles but Pomeranz got out of the inning with no further scoring. In the fourth, the Yankees loaded the bases on a single, double and another walk and two runs scored on ground outs before Hembree came in to get the last out on a tapper in front of the plate but it was 4-0, New York.

Sabathia held the Sox scoreless for four innings but Holaday led off the fifth with a double high off the center field wall and Bogaerts walked. Betts hit a liner which Sabathia caught but then threw wild to first trying for the double play, moving Bogaerts and Holaday to second and third. Hanley Ramirez then hit a homer to drive them in and it was 4-3.

The Sox tied it in the sixth when Shaw, Hill and Bradley hit singles to start the inning before Parker relieved Sabathia and got out of the inning with no more scoring. In the seventh, Ramirez homered again, this time with no one on, and it was 5-4, Boston. It was Ramirez' 28th homer of the year, his fourth of the series and made him 9-16 with nine RBI's in the series and raised his RBI total to 106. The final was 5-4 as the Sox swept the four game series.

After the Yankees made it 4-0 in the fourth, the Red Sox bullpen, with Hembree, Tazawa, Ziegler, Scott, Kelly and Uehara all working, held the Yankees scoreless for 5 1/3 innings. Uehara got the save and Scott got his first win.

Baltimore beat Tampa Bay 2-1 to stay three games back in second place but Toronto lost to Los Angeles to fall four behind, in third. The Sox traveled to Baltimore to start a crucial four game series against the O's on Monday night with a three game lead and just 13 games to play in the season.

CHAPTER 21

THE FINAL ROAD TRIP

SEPTEMBER 19-29

Rick Porcello, 20-4, started against the Orioles' Dylan Bundy, 9-5 , in the first game at Baltimore. The Red Sox got off to a 2-0 lead in the top of the third when Bogaerts singled and Betts hit his 31st homer of the season and eighth against Baltimore, into the left field seats.

After getting the first 11 O's in order, Porcello hit Machado with a pitch and, after the two had words, Trumbo doubled to right and Machado scored when the ball took a bad hop off the wall and got away from Betts in right field and it was 2-1.

Boston added three in the fifth when Benintendi doubled, Pedroia singled to left to drive him in and, with two outs, Ortiz hit his 35th homer of the year deep to right. It was the 538th of his career and gave him 118 RBI's on the year.

It stayed 5-1 until Jones homered for Baltimore in the eighth to make it 5-2 which was the final score.

Porcello pitched a complete game gem for the Sox, giving up just four hits, striking out seven and not walking anyone. He threw just 89 pitches, 65 of them strikes, in gaining his 21st win and strengthening his position as a Cy Young candidate.

Pedroia had two hits to raise his average to .325 and Bradley also had two as the Sox got their five runs on just nine hits.

Toronto beat Seattle and was now tied for second with the O's, but both were four games behind with only 12 to play and the Red Sox magic number to clinch the pennant was now nine. Any combination of nine Boston wins and Baltimore or Toronto losses would eliminate them from the race.

The Red Sox scored first in Game 2 when Mookie Betts led off the third with a bloop single to center, went to third on a ground single up the middle by David Ortiz and scored when Hanley Ramirez hit into a force play at second. It was Betts' 200th hit of the season and Ramirez's 107th RBI. Jackie Bradley got a solo homer in the fourth, his 26th,,, and it was 2-0, Boston.

Eduardo Rodriguez held the O's scoreless until the fifth when Trey Mancini, playing in his first big league game, hit a solo homer to make it 2-1.

In the seventh Ortiz hit his 36th homer to drive in Hernandez and Betts, who had singled and it was 5-1. The Orioles came back with one in the bottom of the seventh when Schoop doubled to lead off the inning, went to third on a ground out and scored on a tapper down the third base line by Hardy against Barnes, who had relieved Rodriguez, with one out.

Ziegler relieved Barnes and got the last out in the seventh and Uehara pitched a perfect eighth. Kimbrel pitched a scoreless ninth despite giving up a two out walk and got his 28th save as the Sox won 5-2.

Rodriguez got his third win with seven losses. Betts had three hits and Bradley, Young and Ortiz all had two each.

The win dropped the Orioles to third place, five games out and the Blue Jays, who beat the Mariners, 10-2, moved into second, four games back.

Before Game 3 with the Orioles, a night game, Toronto had lost to Seattle in an afternoon game, 2-1, so the Sox were up on the second place Jays by 4 ½ with a chance to move five up with a win.

Clay Buchholz, 7-10, started for the Sox and Ubaldo Jiminez, 7-11, for the Orioles. The Orioles scored first in the bottom of the third when Schoop singled to center, moved to second when

Wieters beat out a sacrifice bunt and third when Hardy walked to load the bases. Jones then hit a sacrifice fly to left to make it 1-0, Baltimore, and Buchholz got out of the inning with no further scoring.

In the top of the sixth, Ortiz led off with a walk and Betts hit a ground ball single to left. After Shaw struck out, Brad Brach relieved Jiminez and loaded the bases when Hill beat out a little roller in front of the plate. Bradley then struck out for the second out with the bases still loaded.

Leon then hit a grounder that was fielded by first baseman, Chris Davis, who threw the ball away trying to throw to Brach covering first and Ortiz and Betts scored. The Sox were up 2-1 with runners on second and third and two outs. Andrew Benintendi, up next, hit Brach's first pitch into the fans above the scoreboard in right and it was 5-1 Red Sox. It was the second homer of his big league career.

That was the scoring for the day as Buchholz went seven innings, giving up just the one run on three hits and the Sox won their seventh game in a row. Ziegler pitched a perfect eighth. In the ninth, the Sox brought in rookie Scott, who struck out Davis to start the inning. After he gave up a single to Trumbo, Kimbrel relieved him and got the last two outs for a 5-1 Sox win, all on unearned runs.

Buchholz had perhaps his best game of the season and earned his eighth win, lowering his ERA to 5.00. The Sox have won all four of his starts in September and he has won three of the four with an ERA of 3.97.

Betts got two hits to raise his average to .318 and Benintendi now has 26 hits in his first 25 games with 13 RBI's and 14 runs scored and a .317 average.

The win moved the Sox to five ahead of second place Toronto and six ahead of Baltimore with just ten games to play. Toronto and

Baltimore were still in the lead in the Wild Card race but Houston and Detroit were just one game behind the Orioles for the second spot.

After winning the first three games, the Sox started Price in Game 4 on Thursday night against Chris Tillman, Baltimore's Ace in trying to sweep the series.

The Sox got off to a quick lead in the first when, with two outs. Betts singled, Ortiz walked and Ramirez singled to score Betts and it was 1-0. In the second, Bradley led off with a triple into the right field corner, Leon singled to right to drive him in and, after Tillman struck out Benintendi and got Pedroia to fly out, a single by Holt and a walk to Betts loaded the bases. Ortiz then drew a walk, forcing in Leon and the Sox were up 3-0.

The O's came back in their half of the third on singles by Davis and Machado with one out. After Price struck out Trumbo for the second out, he grooved a pitch to the rookie Mancini, who hit his second home run of his career and second in this series to tie it at 3-3.

The Sox got the lead back in the fifth when Shaw walked, went to second on a wild pitch and scored on Benintendi's single to right. Ramirez hit his 29th homer in the top of the seventh to make it 5-3.

Price held the Orioles scoreless from the third to the seventh and Uehara pitched a scoreless eighth, despite hitting Mancini with a pitch, striking out two batters. Kimbrel pitched a perfect ninth, striking out the first two batters and getting pinch hitter Wieters to fly out to Bradley in center for the last out.

Price improved his record to 17-8 with the win, giving up just the three runs on six hits in seven innings although working with what appeared to be less than his best stuff. Tillman lasted just 1 2/3 innings, leaving after walking in the run in the second.

Kimbrel got his 29th save. Uehara appeared in his eighth game since returning from the disabled list on September 7th and had thrown eight innings since then without giving up a run.

The loss left the Orioles seven games behind, in third place, and 1/2 game out of the Wild Card as Detroit won a double header to move ahead of them. The Blue Jays were idle and fell to 5 ½ games back in second place.

The Sox sweep gave them eight wins in a row and their second four game series sweep in succession. It was the first time the Sox had swept two four game series in succession since July of 1968. They were now 15-5 in the month of September. This game was the fifth consecutive game in which they had scored five runs.

The Sox next traveled to Tampa Bay for a three game series with the Rays who, although mired in last place, had shut out the Yankees the night before and won two of three from the Blue Jays and split a four game series with the Orioles the previous week.

The Rays started Chris Archer in Game 1 against Pomeranz for the Sox. After Bogaerts walked with one out in the first, David Ortiz hit a tape measure homer off the catwalk above the right field seats, to make it 2-0, Red Sox. It was his 37th homer of the year and would be the only runs the Sox would score as Archer went six, giving up no more runs and seven hits while striking out seven.

In the second, the Rays right fielder Mahtook hit a line drive into the seats in left to make it 2-1. Pomeranz went five, giving up just the one run and Kelly, Ross, Barnes, Scott and Ziegler held the Rays scoreless after Pomeranz left and the Sox won 2-1.

Pomeranz got his 11th win with 12 losses and Ziegler got his 22nd save of the year. Archer, who had a 4.02 ERA but had now lost 19 while winning just eight, pitched well in the loss.

In winning their ninth consecutive game, the Sox maintained a 5 ½ game lead over the Blue Jays and a seven game lead over Baltimore, who both won. The magic number for Baltimore was now just two and four for Toronto.

Boston gave starter Rick Porcello, 21-4, the only 21 game winner in baseball, a quick lead in Game 2. Betts led off the second with a single and came all the way around to score on a double by Holt, making it 1-0.

The Rays came back in the third on singles by Casali and Kiermaier and a two out double by Miller scoring them. Dickerson then singled to drive in Miller and it was 3-1, Rays.

In the fourth, Betts walked, stole second and scored when Ramirez singled to right to make it 3-2. In the top of the seventh, the Sox loaded the bases with one out on singles by Ramirez and Holt and a walk to Bradley. Leon then hit a grounder to third and Ramirez was forced at the plate. With two outs and a 3-2 count, Pedroia hit his 14th homer of the year, a grand slam, to put the Sox up 6-3.

Porcello, after having his one typical bad inning, settled down and held the Rays scoreless until being relieved in the seventh with one out.

Farrell used Scott, Ziegler and Ross to get through the seventh and Uehara pitched a scoreless eighth. Kimbrel gave up a two out, solo, homer to Forsythe to make it 6-4 but struck out Kiermaier for the last out and his 30th save as the Sox won, 6-4, for their tenth in a row.

The win clinched a playoff spot for the Sox and reduced their magic number to 3 over Toronto who beat the Yankees 3-0.

In Game 3, with the score tied, 2-2, in the tenth inning, Pedroia singled to lead off the inning. Ortiz then hit a line drive into the right center field gap and Pedroia tried to score all the way from first. The relay to the plate beat him by a good ten feet but was up the first base line a little, causing the catcher, Luke Maile, to have to dive for Pedroia.

In one of the weirdest plays anyone had ever seen, Pedroia slid around him but missed the plate. When he tried to get back to the plate he jumped over Maile and was tagged just before he touched the plate but the ball came out of the glove and he was ruled safe. After replay, the safe call was upheld and the Sox were ahead 3-2.

In the last of the tenth, Joe Kelly, who had come in in the eighth in relief, held the Rays scoreless, despite giving up two singles and the Red Sox had won their 11th in a row.

Red Sox pitchers set major league records for strikeouts despite needing ten innings to win the game. Eduardo Rodriguez started and went 5 1/3 innings, giving up just one run on three hits and striking out 13, the last six he faced in order. Heath Hembree replaced him and struck out the next five in a row, making it 11 strikeouts in a row, the most in baseball history.

Barnes, who replaced Hembree, got one strikeout and Kelly got two more before the end of the ninth to make it 21 strikeouts in nine innings, the most ever in baseball history. To add to the total, Kelly got two more in the tenth to give the Sox 23 strikeouts for the game.

The Sox had scored in the first when Bogaerts walked, Ortiz singled to right and Betts singled to center to drive in Bogaerts and make it 1-0. The Rays got one in the second on a Mahtook double, a walk to Dickerson and a single by Maile to load the bases. Shaffer then hit a sac fly to center tying it at 1-1.

In the Sox third, Pedroia homered to left to put the Sox up 2-1. It was his 15th homer of the season and his second in two games.

In the Rays eighth, with Barnes pitching, Forsythe singled to lead off and break the string of strikeouts. It was the first ball the Rays had put in play since the second inning. Longoria then walked and Abad replaced Barnes on the mound for the Sox. He immediately gave up a single to Miller tying the score and Kelly relieved him.

Kelly got out of the inning and went the rest of the way for the win, his fourth, and the team's 11th in a row. Pedroia, apparently out of his brief slump had two hits for the second game in a row, giving him 195 on the year.

The Blue Jays came from behind to beat the Yankees but the Sox win reduced their magic number to two and eliminated the Orioles from the race for the division.

Boston now traveled to New York for a three game series with the Yankees starting on Tuesday, after a day off.

On Monday, after losing three in a row to the Blue Jays, the Yankees came from behind 3-2, and scored five in the top of the ninth to beat Toronto, 7-5. The Toronto loss dropped them to six games behind the Sox and reduced the Red Sox magic number to clinch the division to one.

After striking out Gardner to start Game 1 against the Yankees, David Price gave up a single to Ellsbury and a homer to Sanchez, the rookie catcher's 20th in 50 games, and the Sox were down 2-0. Romine added a solo homer in the fifth and it was 3-0.

Luis Cessa, the former infielder turned pitcher,who started for the Yankees, kept Boston scoreless through five. In the sixth, Benintendi hit a dribbler in front of the plate and Cessa threw wild to first and Benintendi ended up on second. Pedroia then singled him in and Bogaerts doubled to left to put men on second and third with no outs. After Ortiz struck out, Betts grounded out, scoring Bogaerts and Ramirez struck out to end the inning, 3-2, New York.

Gregorius hit a solo homer for New York in the last half of the sixth and it was 4-2.

Hill, batting for Holt, led off the Sox seventh with a solo homer to left. After Bradley singled, Leon sacrificed him to second and, with two outs, Pedroia drove him in. Bogaerts singled to put two men on but Ortiz hit a little roller to short for the third out and it was 4-4.

In the last of the seventh, Romine singled and Price gave up his third homer of the game, to Austin, to make it 6-4. Gardner then singled and Ellsbury lined out. Ziegler replaced Price and got a double play and the inning ended with the score 6-4.

Neither team scored in the eighth. In the ninth, with Clippard on the mound for New York, Benintendi doubled to right center and Pedroia walked to put the tying runs on base with one out. Bogaerts popped to short and Ortiz struck out, the third time in four innings he had come up with runners in scoring position and done nothing.

Price got the loss, giving up six runs on 12 hits in 6 1/3 innings. Bogaerts had three hits, and Pedroia and Benintendi had two each as the Sox 10 hit attack could produce just four runs.

Toronto beat Baltimore 5-1 to keep the Sox from clinching and drop Baltimore to just one game ahead of Detroit for the second Wild Card spot with five games to play.

Clay Buchholz started Game 2 against the Yankees Bryan Mitchell. The games was scoreless through seven innings with Buchholz going six and giving up just one hit and Mitchell throwing seven on just two hits. Ziegler pitched a 1-2-3 seventh for the Sox and, at the end of seven, it was still 0-0.

In the top of the eighth, Adam Warren came on in relief for the Yankees and Leon, leading off, reached on an error by second baseman Castro and Pedroia hit a ground rule double to right. Bogaerts lined out to third and Ortiz was intentionally walked to load the bases with one out. Betts then doubled to left to score two and Ramirez was intentionally walked to load the bases again. Ex-Red Sox pitcher, Tommy Layne, came in to relieve Warren. With Jackie Bradley at bat, Ortiz scored on a passed ball and it was 3-0, Red Sox.

Uehara held the Yankees scoreless in the eighth and Kimbrel came on for the ninth. He gave up a single to Gardner then walked Ellsbury, Sanchez and McCann in order to force in a run and it was 3-1. Kelly came on in relief of Kimbrel with the bases loaded and no outs. He struck out Castro and got Gregorius on a pop out to Bogaerts at short. Mark Teixeira, playing in the last week of his career, before retirement, then hit a walk off, grand slam homer to right to win the game 5-3.

Despite the discouraging, walk off loss, the Sox still clinched the pennant as Toronto had lost to Baltimore 3-2 to eliminate themselves. The Red Sox had a celebration in their clubhouse after watching the Yankees celebrate their walk off win on the field. The Jays and Orioles remained numbers one and two in the Wild Card race with Detroit one game behind the Orioles.

In Game 3, the Red Sox rested some of their starters, and after C. C. Sabathia had struck out Hill, Benintendi and Bogaerts to start the game, the Yankees got one in their half of the first. Ellsbury walked, stole second and scored when Castro doubled to left.

In the Sox fourth Bogaerts tied it at 1-1 with a homer to left. That was all the Red Sox scoring for the night as Sabathia went 7 1/3 innings for his ninth win.

The Yankees got another in the fifth when Hicks led off with a bunt pop single that Red Sox starter, Henry Owens, was unable to field. After two were out, Ellsbury doubled to center to score Hicks and Hembree came in to relieve Owens who hadn't pitched badly and had gone 4 2/3 giving up just the two runs on four hits.

Hembree got out of the inning but gave up a single to Castro and a walk to Headley in the sixth and was replaced by Scott. He gave up a single to McCann, loading the bases and then walked Austin to force in a run. With Gardner batting, Headley scored on a wild pitch and it was 4-1. The Yankees added a run in the eighth when Hicks doubled in McCann to make the final 5-1.

The Yankees had swept the Sox but the Sox were the Division winner. They would open the ALDS the following Thursday but their opponent was yet unknown.

If Toronto and Baltimore won the Wild Card slots, the Sox would have to play the Indians, assuming Texas continued to have the best record in the league, because a Division winner cannot play a team from its own division in the first round of the playoffs.

CHAPTER 22

THE FINAL SERIES

SEPTEMBER 30-OCTOBER 2

Toronto came into Boston for the last three games of the season. The Red Sox were one game ahead of the Indians for the second best record in the American League so they needed any combination of three wins and Indian losses in the last three games to have the home field advantage in the ALDS.

Each night of the series, the game was preceded by a celebration of David Ortiz' contributions to the team, the Boston community and the Dominican Republic to recognize him in his last three regular season games at Fenway. Packed houses watched the ceremonies and Ortiz and his foundation were the recipients of many gifts, including the naming of a bridge after him.

The Sox got a run in the first inning of Game 1 against Toronto when Holt, playing third and batting second and apparently the Sox choice for their third baseman in the playoffs, walked, went to second on a wild pitch and scored on a single to left by Ortiz.

It stayed 1-0 until the top of the fifth, when Red Sox starter Porcello gave up a lead off double to the ninth hitter Travis. Carrera then bunted and beat it out and Travis scored on a sac fly by Donaldson. Bautista hit a homer to left and it was 3-1, Toronto.

It was 3-1 until the last of the eighth when Benintendi doubled and Pedroia hit a little tapper in front of the plate. The Jays catcher, Martin, threw the ball away allowing Benintendi to score and putting Pedroia on second. Pedroia got credit for a single, his 201st hit of the season. Betts then singled to drive in Pedroia and Ortiz hit his 38th homer of the year into the seats in right field and it was 5-3. It was his 500th homer as a member of the Red Sox, including post season play, and gave him 127 RBI's on the season. Ziegler had pitched a scoreless seventh and Uehara, despite giving up a walk and a double, a scoreless eighth. Kimbrel came in for the ninth and had control problems again, walking two before getting out of the inning with no scoring for his 31st save. Ziegler got the win, bringing his record to 4-6.

The Indians beat Kansas City 7-2 so the Red Sox magic number for the home field advantage with Cleveland was lowered to two.

Rodriguez started Game 2 for the Sox against Happ for the Jays. Boston got two quick runs in the last of the first when Happ walked the bases full with two outs and Young singled to make it 2-0, Red Sox.

Rodriguez returned the favor, walking the bases full in the second and then giving up a single to Pillar to tie the score at 2-2. It was 2-2 after five and Rodriguez walked Martin to lead off the Jays sixth and was replaced by Barnes who got a fly out before walking pinch hitter Saunders and giving up another run scoring single by Pillar.

The Sox tied it in the eighth when Betts led off the inning with a double to right. Ramirez then walked and Holt, batting for Young, hit into a double play and Betts moved to third. With Bradley batting, the Jays Closer, Osuna, balked and Betts scored, tying the game at 3-3.

In the top of the ninth, Kimbrel came on in relief, and walked Saunders. Pompey came in to run for him and Pillar sacrificed him to second. He then went to third on a wild pitch and scored when Carrera flied out to left to put the Jays up to stay, 4-3.

Osuna put the Red Sox down in order in the ninth for his fourth win and Kimbrel's loss made his record 2-6. All four Toronto runs were score by runners who reached base on walks. Kelly had pitched the seventh and eighth for Boston allowing no base runners and striking out the last four batters he faced before being relieved by Kimbrel whose ERA now went to 3.40. Betts got two hits in the game, giving him 214 on the year.

The Sox fell ½ game behind the Indians in the race for the home field advantage in the ALDS which would start Thursday. The Jays clinched a tie for the Wild Card berth by the win.

Needing a win in the last game of the season to earn the home field advantage against Cleveland, Boston sent David Price against the Jays' Aaron Sanchez, 14-2. Sanchez no hit the Sox through 6 2/3 innings before Hanley Ramirez hit a homer to right with two out in the seventh. Bradley followed with a single but the Sox were all done scoring for the day and the regular season.

The Jays had gotten a solo homer from Travis in the fifth so Hanley's homer made it 1-1. It went to the eighth still 1-1 and Ziegler, who had come in to relieve Barnes and get the last out of the seventh, gave up a single to Donaldson, walked Encarnacion and, after getting a third to first double play erasing Donaldson, allowed Tulowitzki to single driving in Encarnacion with what would be the winning run.

Osuna came in with one on in the eighth and got a five out save despite giving up a walk and single with two out in the ninth. It was his 36th save of the season.

Ramirez' homer gave him 30 for the year and increased his total RBI's to 110. With Ortiz and Betts both over 30 homers and 100 RBI's, it was the first time in Red Sox history that they had three players with over 30 homers and 100 RBI's. Price pitched well in what was a tuneup for the playoffs, going five innings and giving up just one run on four hits.

The loss gave the Indians the home field advantage in the ALDS. Detroit lost earlier, giving the Jays the second Wild Card spot.

Toronto would play the Orioles in the Wild Card Game Tuesday night for the right to meet Texas in the ALDS. The Wild Card

Game in the National League would have the Giants at the Mets. In the American League Division Series the Rangers host the Wild Card winner and the Indians host the Red Sox. In the National League the Cubs host the Wild Card winner and the Nationals host the Dodgers.

In the American League Wild Card Game, played October 4, at the Rogers Centre in Toronto, the Blue Jays beat the Orioles, 5-2, in 11 innings on a three run, walk off home run by Edward Encarnacion. The Jays would now face the Texas Rangers in the League Division Series.

Over in the National League, the next night, the Giants beat the Mets, 3-0, at Citi Field in New York on another three run homer, this time by Conor Gillaspie, the number eight hitting, third baseman, in the ninth inning. The Giants Madison Bumgarner had pitched a four hit complete game shutout for the win. The Giants would meet the Cubs in the Division Series.

CHAPTER 23

THE DIVISION SERIES

The Sox, after finding themselves riding their 11 game winning streak to the brink of winning the Eastern Division, had lost five of their last six during the last week of the season. With three days off before beginning play at Cleveland on Thursday night, the question was, could they regain the form they had shown all year as they began the playoffs?

They opened up at Progressive Field, on October 6, with Rick Porcello, 22-4, on the mound against Trevor Bauer, 12-8, for the Indians.

The Sox got off to a quick start, scoring in the first when Pedroia led off with a double into the right field corner. Holt, starting at third base, then singled to right with Pedroia stopping at third. After Betts struck out and Ortiz fouled out to Mike Napoli at first, Ramirez doubled, scoring Pedroia but Holt was thrown out at the plate on a relay from center fielder, Tyler Naquin to shortstop Francisco Lindor to Roberto Perez at the plate.

In the last of the second, third baseman Jose Ramirez doubled to lead off and scored when right fielder Lonnie Chisenhall singled to center to make it 1-1. Benintendi led off the third with a solo homer in his first playoff at bat to put the Sox back ahead, 2-1.

In the Indians' third, Porcello gave up solo homers to Perez, second baseman Jason Kipnis and Lindor, with Kipnis and Lindor going back to back, to make it 4-2.

Leon hit a lead off homer in the fifth to make it 4-3 but the Indians got it back in the last of the inning when Perez singled, went to second on a fly out and scored on Kipnis' single and it was 5-3.

Holt led off the eighth with a homer for the Sox but that was all the scoring they got as the game ended 5-4. Bauer and three relievers, despite giving up 10 hits, including five doubles and three homers, had struck out 14 Red Sox batters, including Pedroia, Bogaerts and Bradley three times each and the Sox were down one game to none.

Porcello had lasted just 4 1/3 innings giving up all five runs and took the loss. Ex Red Sox pitcher, Andrew Miller, who pitched two scoreless innings, got the win. Holt had three hits, including a homer and double, Ramirez had two doubles and Benintendi had two hits, including a homer. The rest of the lineup could manage only two singles and a double.

A crowd of 37,762 watched the game which took 3 hours and 33 minutes to play.

The Indians started their Ace Corey Kluber, 18-9, in Game 2 against David Price, 17-9. Price had trouble from the beginning, giving up four runs in the second on singles by designated hitter Carlos Santana, Ramirez and left fielder Brandon Guyer and a three run homer to right by Chisenhall.

Meanwhile, Kluber was having no trouble with the suddenly anemic bats of the Red Sox as he went seven scoreless innings giving up just three hits, all singles, while striking out seven.

Cleveland added a run in the fourth, after Price gave up a single and walk and was relieved by Barnes, who gave up an RBI single to Kipnis before getting out of the inning. They got another, unearned run, in the sixth, when Pedroia booted a routine double play ball and center fielder Rajai Davis hit a sac fly to score the sixth run and make the final 6-0.

Kluber got the win and Price took the loss. Dan Otero came in for the Indians after Kluber had put two on with a walk and hit batter with no outs in the eighth and got Pedroia, Betts and Holt to end the threat and Bryan Shaw got the Sox 1-2-3 in the ninth.

A crowd of 37,842 watched the game which lasted 3 hours and 19 minutes. The teams were off on Saturday and would return to Boston for Game 3 on Sunday with the Sox facing elimination.

The Blue Jays had beaten the Rangers in Texas in the first two games of their Division Series, 10-1 and 5-3. The Jays had six home runs in the two games by six different batters to push Texas to the brink of elimination going back to Toronto.

On Friday night, after the American League second games, the first National League Division Series games were played. The Los Angeles Dodgers, behind their Ace, Clayton Kershaw, beat the Washington Nationals and their Ace Max Scherzer, 4-3. In the other National League game, former Red Sox Ace, Jon Lester, pitched eight innings of shutout, five hit ball, as the Chicago Cubs beat the San Francisco Giants 1-0 and Johnny Cueto on an eighth inning homer by 23 year old third baseman Javier Baez.

On Saturday, the Cubs won their second in a row, beating the Giants 5-2. Travis Wood of the Cubs, won the game in relief and also hit a home run off George Kontos in the fourth inning to become the second relief pitcher to homer in post season history. The only other homer by a reliever was New York Giants' pitcher Rosy Ryan's round tripper against the Washington Senators in the 1924 World Series.

The second game between the Dodgers and Nationals at Washington was postponed due to rain.

Game 3 between the Red Sox and Indians would have to wait another day as Monday saw a steady rain all day in Boston causing the game to be postponed.

While the Red Sox were idle, Toronto completed their rout of the Rangers, winning the third in a row 7-6 to end that series and earn the right to face the Sox or Indians in the ALCS. The Jays hit two more homers giving them eight in three games and won the game in the tenth when Josh Donaldson scored from second on an error. In the National League, the Nationals tied their series with the Dodgers at one each with a 5-2 win. Nationals catcher Jose Lobaton, who hit only three homers during the regular season, homered in the fourth inning with two on to put the Nationals up 3-2 and the bullpen did the rest, shutting out the Dodgers the rest of the way for the win.

On Monday night, in clear but cold conditions, at Fenway, the Sox and Indians finally took the field for Game 3. The Sox started Clay Buchholz, 8-10, against the Indians' Josh Tomlin, 13-9. Although Buchholz had had a rocky season, he had come on in September winning three and losing none in five starts and compiling a 3.14 ERA in 28 2/3 innings while the Sox had won four of his five starts.

Despite giving up four hits in the first three innings, Buchholz held the Indians scoreless while Tomlin was giving up just one hit and blanking the Sox.

In the top of the fourth, Ramirez singled to right to lead off the inning for the Tribe. Buchholz then walked Chisenhall and Coco Crisp sacrificed them to second and third with a perfect bunt in front of the plate. Naquin then singled to right and it was 2-0, Indians. Buchholz got the next two batters to end the inning.

After the Sox went 1-2-3 in their half of the fourth, Drew Pomeranz replaced Buchholz and got the Indians in order in the fifth with two strikeouts.

In the last of the fifth, with one out, Bogaerts lined a single to center and Benintendi followed with a double scoring Bogaerts and it was 2-1. Tomlin struck out Leon and got Bradley to ground to first for the last out.

In the Indians' sixth, with Pomeranz still on the mound, Ramirez drew a lead off walk and Chisenhall sacrificed him to second. Coco Crisp then homered deep to left and it was 4-2, Cleveland.

Pedroia led off the Sox sixth with a ground single to center and former Sox reliever Andrew Miller replaced Tomlin on the mound. Miller struck out Hill, batting for Holt, who had been 4-10 in the series until then. Betts then doubled to center to put runners on second and third with one out and Ortiz and Ramirez coming up. Ortiz flied out to center, scoring Pedroia and Miller struck out Ramirez to end the inning with the score 4-2, Indians.

Kelly got the Indians in order in the seventh and Miller, despite a walk to Young, hitting for Benintendi, who had been 3-9 in the series until then, got through the seventh unscored on and it was still 4-2 going to the eighth.

Uehara relieved Kelly in the eighth and got the Indians 1-2-3, making it eight in a row since Kelly came in. In the last of the eighth, Bryan Shaw replaced Miller on the mound for the Indians and struck out Pedroia to lead off the inning.

Shaw came in to pinch hit for Hill and singled to right. Betts then grounded to third, forcing Shaw at second for the second out. Cody Allen replaced Shaw pitching for the Indians. Ortiz walked and Ramirez lined a single to left, scoring Betts and putting the tying run, Ortiz, on second. After Marco Hernandez came in to run for Ortiz, Bogaerts lined to second for the final out of the inning and the game went to the ninth, 4-3 Cleveland.

Kimbrel pitched a perfect ninth for the Sox getting the Indians on two strikeouts and a foul pop, making it 11 batters in a row retired by Red Sox relievers..

In the last of the ninth, Young flied to left and Leon struck out and the Sox were down to their last out. Jackie Bradley lined a single to right and Pedroia drew a walk and the tying run was on second with Shaw at the plate and two out. With the count three balls and two strikes, Shaw flied out to right and the Red Sox season was over.

CHAPTER 24

THE REST OF THE POST SEASON

While the Red Sox were being swept by the the Indians, the Blue Jays were sweeping the Rangers in three games with seven different players homering for the Jays, including Edward Encarnacion, who had two. The Jays pitching held the Rangers offense to ten runs and posted a 3.21 ERA compared to Texas' 6.18.

Marco Estrada had gotten the Jays off to a good start in Game 1, going 8 1/3 innings and giving up just one run on four hits for the 10-1 win. J. A Happ pitched Game 2 and gave up just one run in five innings while the Jays were winning, 5-3. Aaron Sanchez did not fare as well in Game 3, giving up six runs in 5 2/3 innings in the Jays 7-6 win. That game went to ten innings, tied 6-6, and Josh Donaldson scored the winning run on a throwing error in the last of the tenth.

In the National League, the Cubs handled the Giants easily, winning three games to one. Former Red Sox pitcher and fan favorite, Jon Lester, pitched Game 1 for the Cubs and shut out the Giants for eight innings on five hits as the Cubs won, 1-0. In Game 4, John Lackey, another former Red Sox pitcher started Game 4 but lasted just four innings as the Cubs got four in the ninth to win, 6-5. Former Red Sox catcher David Ross homered in the third for the Cubs.

In the other NLDS, the Dodgers needed all five games to eliminate the Nationals. After Clayton Kershaw, the Dodgers Ace, won Game 1, going five innings and giving up three runs on eight hits as the Dodgers won 4-3, he started Game 4 and lasted 6 2/3 innings, giving up five runs on seven hits but not getting a decision in the Dodgers 6-5 win. He came back in Game 5, entering the game with the Dodgers up 4-3, with one out and two on, in the ninth and got the second and third out on a pop out and a strikeout to earn the save and put the Dodgers in the NLCS.

Another former Red Sox pitcher, Rich Hill had started Game 2, giving up four runs on six hits in the Dodgers 5-2 loss. In the same game, another Red Sox alumni, the Nationals, Mark Melancon, got the save, pitching a scoreless ninth. With one out, he gave up a single but then struck out Adrian Gonzalez and got Josh Reddick on a ground out to second for the save. Of course, both Gonzalez and Reddick were also former Red Sox players. Melancon made four appearances in the Series, pitching 4 1/3 innings, striking out eight and not allowing a run.

The American League Championship Series, with the Indians facing the Blue Jays, began on October 14, in Cleveland's Progressive Field. The NLCS, pitting the Cubs against the Dodgers, began in historic Wrigley Field the next night.

In Game 1 of the ALCS, in Cleveland's Progressive Field, Corey Kluber started and Andrew Miller and Cody Allen took over from the seventh on and the trio shut out the Toronto offense on seven hits and no runs for a 2-0 win. In Game 2, Josh Tomlin started for the Indians and Bryan Shaw, Miler and Allen finished from the sixth in a 2-1 victory for Cleveland, holding Toronto to three hits.

With Cleveland up, two games to none, the scene shifted to the Rogers Center and the Indians' pitching, with Trevor Bauer starting and six relievers, including Shaw, Allen and Miller from the fifth on, held the Jays to two runs on seven hits for a 4-2 win which left the Indians on the verge of elimination with two home games coming up.

Aaron Sanchez started for the Jays and with relief help, the Jays held the Indians to two hits and one run and won 5-1 to prevent elimination.

In Game 5, Ryan Merritt started for the Indians and, even though he was ahead, 3-0, after 4 1/3, when he gave up a single in the fifth, Francona brought in Shaw in relief and he Miller and Allen held the Jays scoreless for the last 4 2/3 for a 3-0 victory and the

Series win. The Indians, who had not won a World Series since 1948 were going to the World Series.

Andrew Miller, another former Red Sox player, who was in four of the five games in relief and pitched 7 2/3 innings, without giving up a run and striking out 14, was named Most Valuable Player of the ALCS.

Game 1 of the NLCS was tied at 3-3 going to the last of the eighth. The Cubs had the bases loaded, with two out, when pinch hitter Miguel Montero hit a grand slam to put the Cubs up 7-3 and Dexter Fowler followed with a solo homer and the Cubs won 8-4. In Game 2, Kershaw and Kenley Jansen shut out the Cubs 1-0 on two hits and the Series went to Los Angeles.

In Game 3, Rich Hill and three relievers shut out the Cubs again, this time on just four hits and the Dodgers were up two games to one with the next two games at home. The Cubs came back and found their bats, winning Game 4, 10-2, to even the Series again.

In Game 5, the Cubs got five runs in the eighth inning again for another 8-4 win behind John Lester, who went seven innings giving up one run on five hits for the win. With the Cubs up 3-2, the Series went back to Chicago.

Kyle Hendricks completely stifled the Dodgers in Game 6, pitching 7 2/3 innings of shutout ball, allowing only two hits and Aroldis Chapman finished the shut out for a 5-0 win and the Cubs were on the way to the World Series for the first time since 1945 and were looking for their first World Series win in 108 years.

The following article appeared in my column, Baseball World in the Biddeford, Maine, Journal Tribune on October 30, 2016.

TERRY FRANCONA'S SUCCESS

Terry Francona did it again. He took a team decimated by injury, and decimated is probably not a strong enough word for the damage caused his team by injuries during the year, and took them to the World Series. Red Sox fans don't have to be told that Terry is one of the most effective managers in baseball.

He works his magic quietly, without fanfare. No one has ever called him innovative or radical in his approach to managing and in his managerial decisions. Yet, in his approach to his pitching staff, particularly during the ALDS and ALCS this year, he may have changed the manner in which baseball managers use their pitching staffs in the future.

His Cleveland Indians had picked up Andrew Miller from the New York Yankees on July 31 of this year. Miller had been in 26 games with the Indians during the rest of the regular season, pitching 29 innings with a 1.55 ERA and three saves while striking out 46 batters in those 29 innings.

He had been used as a set up man, similar to the way in which he had been used in New York when he, Aroldis Chapman and Dellin Betances had been the strongest back end of the bullpen in baseball, before being broken up in the Yankees Rebuilding Fire Sale of 2016. With the Indians, in the 26 times he had come in in relief, he was called upon eight times in the eighth inning and 18 times in the ninth but had never come in before the eighth.

In the fifth inning of Game 1 of the ALDS, with the Indians up on the Red Sox, 4-2, the Indian starter, right handed Trevor Bauer, gave up a lead off home run to Sandy Leon to make it 4-3. Bauer then got the next two batters out. With the left handed hitting Brock Holt due up, Francona brought in left handed Miller to pitch to Holt. The fact that, if he got one more out, Bauer would qualify for the win if the Indians eventually went on to win, which often colors a manager's decision, apparently did not matter to Terry. He, obviously and rightly, decided that the game was more important than Bauer's won/loss record.

In a perfect world, Miller would have gotten Holt for the third out but Holt doubled and Betts walked and the bases were loaded. Miller then struck out the left handed Ortiz to end the inning. Miller got the Sox 1-2-3, with two strike outs in the sixth and got the first two batters in the seventh. With the right handed Pedroia coming up, Francona brought in right handed Bryan Shaw to pitch to him and he got him on a ground out.

Shaw gave up a homer to Holt to lead off the eighth and got the next out. Francona brought in his Closer, Cody Allen, who despite giving up two hits, struck out four and held the Sox scoreless as the Indians won, 5-4.

In Game 3, ahead 4-1 in the sixth inning, Indian starter, Josh Tomlin gave up a lead off single to Pedroia. Francona went to Miller early again, and he struck out Hill but Betts doubled and Ortiz hit a line drive to right that was caught, scoring Pedroia but Miller struck out Ramirez to end the inning, ahead 4-2. He held the Sox scoreless in the seventh and Shaw and Allen took it the rest of the way.

Francona had brought in Miller in the fifth and sixth inning for the first time since he joined the team. While most managers will hold a fireballing setup man or Closer like Miller until the end of the game, Francona brought him in when he felt he needed him most. He used Miller, Shaw and Allen in the same way in the ALCS, bringing them in as needed, even bringing in Closer Allen before Miller in Game 3 and Shaw in the sixth of Game 2 and the fifth of Game 5.

Using your best relievers to put out fires in the earlier innings instead of saving them for the finish is an old concept that got lost in the evolution from pitchers that went complete games to specialists that pitch only certain innings, like Closers and set up men. The fact is that a run scored in the sixth inning counts just as much and hurts just as much as one scored in the ninth, so why not prevent that early run while you can by using your most effective pitcher at that point.

In the old days, which most of you don't remember but I do, relievers were sometimes called Firemen because they were brought in as needed 'to put out fires' no matter what the inning. In fact, Joe Page, a left hander, who pitched for the Yankees from 1944 until 1950, was called The Fireman.

In 1947 with the Yankees and Dodgers matched up in Game 7 of the World Series, the Yankees got two in the last of the fourth to go up 3-2 after four innings. Page came in to start the fifth and got the next 13 batters in a row until giving up a single to Eddie Mixsis with one out in the ninth. He then got the next batter to hit into a double play and the Yankees had won the series. Yankee Manager Buckie Harris had not waited for his pitcher to get in trouble to use his Fireman. He got the lead and used him when he needed him for the win.

In 1949, the Red Sox were ahead of the Yankees by one game with two to play in the regular season. The Red Sox were ahead 2-0 with the bases loaded in the third. Yankee Manager Casey Stengel brought in Page, his Fireman, in relief. Although he walked the first two batters, forcing in two runs to make it 4-0, he one hit the Red Sox for the next 6 2/3 innings while his team mates were scoring five with the big hit a go ahead homer in the eighth by Johnny Lindell and the Yankees won 5-4. The Sabre Project calls Page's performance that day ' one of the greatest clutch pitching performance in history'.

Stengel had seen the need to stop it where it was and brought the Fireman in early. Unfortunately, for Red Sox fans, Vic Raschi beat the Sox, 5-3, the next day and the Yankees won the pennant.

In the playoffs, because of the short duration, each game is so much more important than in the 162 game season and this magnifies the importance of each run. Francona's success may have long reaching effects on the use of those elite pitchers who have been used solely at the end of games.

CARL H. JOHNSON
October 30, 2016

CHAPTER 25

THE WORLD SERIES

With the Cubs, who hadn't won a Series in 108 years and the Indians, who hadn't won one in 68 years, facing each other, it was sure that one of the droughts would be broken.

The Cubs had had the best record in baseball with 103 wins and 68 losses while the Indians were 94-67, nine games worse, but because the American League had won the All Star Game, the Indians had the home field advantage, so Game 1 was played in Progressive Field in Cleveland.

The Indians got off to a great start at home, winning Game 1 behind Corey Kluber and, with late inning help from Miller and Allen, shut out the Cubs on seven hits to win 6-0 and go up one game.

The Cubs came right back in Game 2, with Jake Arrietta, Mike Montgomery and Aroldis Chapman holding the Indians to one run on four hits for a Series evening 5-1 win.

In Game 3, in Wrigley Field, Josh Tomlin was pitching well for the Indians but, in the fifth, with two out and a runner on first, and the score 0-0, Miller replaced him and Miller, Shaw and Allen finished up a 1-0 victory, with Miller getting the win. The only run scored in the seventh when Coco Crisp, another former Red Sox player, pinch hitting for Miller, drove in what turned out to be the winning run.

The Indians won Game 4, 7-2, behind Corey Kluber, who went six innings, giving up just one run, and Miller pitched the seventh and eighth, giving up a run on a Dexter Fowler homer, the first run he had given up in the Playoffs. Dan Otero pitched the ninth to finish it up and the Indians needed just one more win to clinch the Series with three left.

The Cubs started their Ace, John Lester, who went six innings, giving up just two runs on four hits and left ahead 3-2 in Game 5. The Cubs had scored three in the fourth to go ahead with the third and eventual winning run being driven in on a sac fly by another former Red Sox player, David Ross. After Carl Edwards relieved Lester in the seventh and got just one out, Chapman relieved him with the score 3-2 and pitched the last 2 2/3 shutout innings for the longest save of his career.

It was now three games to two, Indians, going back to Cleveland, with the Cubs still one game away from elimination.

The Cubs tied the Series at three games with a 9-3 win in Game 6, scoring their nine runs on 13 hits while Jake Arrietta and four relievers held the Indians to three. The Cubs had gotten three in the first inning when Kris Bryant hit a solo homer and two more scored when a pop fly off the bat of Addison Russell fell between two fielders for a tainted double. In the third, Russell hit a grand slam homer to put the Cubs up 7-0 and that was it.

The Cubs had taken the Series to six games by winning two in a row after being down 3-2. How much more exciting could it get? Two teams, who hadn't won a World Series between them in 76 years, both of whom were original members of their leagues, not only playing each other in the World Series, but going to a seventh game.

The Cubs started Kyle Hendricks on the mound and Corey Kluber started for the Indians in Game 7 at Cleveland. Dexter Fowler, the Cubs lead off hitter, hit Kluber's 2-1 pitch high over the center field wall to put the Cubs up 1-0 after one batter.

The Indians came back and tied it in the third when Coco Crisp doubled to left, moved to third on a sacrifice bunt by Perez and scored on Santana's single to right.

The Cubs added two in the fourth to go up 3-1. Bryant singled to left, Rizzo was hit by a pitch and Zobrist grounded to first, forcing Rizzo at second. Russell then flied to center, scoring Bryant from third and Contreras doubled to center to score Zobrist.

They added two more in the fifth. Baez led off the inning with a home run to right center and Miller relieved Kluber. After two were out, Bryant walked and Rizzo singled to right and, by the time the ball came back in, Rizzo had scored, making it 5-1, Cubs.

In the Indians sixth, former Red Sox player, David Ross, homered to deep center in what would be his last at bat of his career, to make it 5-2.

It went to the last of the eighth, 5-2. With two outs and Lester, who had relieved Hendricks in the fifth, on the mound, Ramirez beat out a grounder to short. Chapman relieved Lester, his third appearance in three games, including his 2 2/3 innings in Game 5. Brandon Guyer met him with a double to right center, scoring Ramirez and Rajai Davis hit a 2-2 pitch over the left field wall to tie the game at 5-5.

It had been raining for a while and time was called and the tarp put on the field and it began to look like the game might not end that night. However, the delay lasted just 17 minutes and the teams were back at it.

It went to the tenth 5-5 and Kyle Schwarber led off with a single to right. Albert Almora ran for him and moved to second when Bryant flied out deep to center. Rizzo was walked intentionally with one out and Zobrist followed with a double to right, scoring Almora. Russell was intentionally walked to load the bases. Miguel Montero, the Cubs third catcher of the day, then hit a ground single into left to score Rizzo and make it 7-5 Cubs.

In the last of the tenth, the Indians came back against Carl Edwards, who replaced Chapman. After he got the first two men out, Guyer walked and went to second on defensive indifference. Rajai Davis came through again with a single to center, scoring

Guyer and it was 7-6. Maddon then brought in Mike Montgomery to replace Edwards. Montgomery got Martinez to ground to third and the Cubs had their first World Series win in 108 years.

From beginning to end, it was one of the most exciting Post Seasons in baseball history and Game 7 of the World Series was one of the most dramatic finishes in years.

Unfortunately for Big Papi and the Kids, their season had ended 23 days too early.

CHAPTER 26

THE FUTURE

The 2016 Red Sox, after the team had finished in last place, two years in a row, may have given the baseball world a glimpse of what is to come in the immediate future. This group had a team batting average of .282, the best in all of baseball, a team ERA of 4.00, the fourth best in the American League, behind the Indians, Blue Jays and Mariners, and the fifth best fielding percentage in all of baseball and the third best in the American League.

After the season was over the Awards started coming in for the Red Sox stars of 2016. Mookie Betts won the Gold Glove as the best defensive right fielder. Then Rick Porcello was picked as the Players' Choice Award winner as the Best Pitcher in baseball.

Silver Slugger Awards went to Designated Hitter David Ortiz, Right Fielder Mookie Betts and Shortstop Xander Bogaerts as the best hitters at their positions.

The Wilson Awards for Best Defensive Player in all of baseball at their position went to Dustin Pedroia at Second Base and Mookie Betts in Right Field.

On November 15, sixty years after the first Cy Young was given, Rick Porcello became the fourth Red Sox pitcher to receive the Award. In one of the closest votes ever, he beat out Detroit's Justin Verlander and Cleveland's Corey Kluber. Verlander, with a 16-9 record and a 3.04 ERA this year had previously won the Award in 2011. Kluber was 18-9 this year with a 3.14 ERA and had won the Award in 2014.

Porcello, of course, won 22 and lost just 4, including winning eight of his last nine decisions, down the stretch, this year. He had a 3.15 ERA, and had averaged just 1.3 walks per nine innings and 6 2/3 innings per start for 33 starts while being a major reason the Sox won the Eastern Division before losing in the Playoffs. After the debacle that was 2015, his first year with the Red Sox, when Porcello won just 9 and lost 15 for a .375 win/loss percentage, he reached the potential he had shown when with the Detroit Tigers, pitching behind Max Scherzer, Justin Verlander and even David Price.

Only one pitcher in American League history has ever won a Cy Young Award after having a lower win/loss percentage the previous year. Jim Palmer, the Orioles Hall of Famer, won the Award in 1975 with a 23-11 record after posting a 7-12 record for a .368 win/loss percentage in 1974. He had won the Award with a 22-9 record, in 1973, the year before his terrible 1974 record and won it again in 1976 with a 22-13 record.

While with Detroit, from 2009 to 2014, Porcello had won 10 or more games every year and has now won 107 and lost 82 and has started 27 or more games every year for eight years. At age 27, he should have many productive years ahead of him and he is under contract with the Sox until he becomes eligible for Free Agency in 2020. The $95.+ million dollar, five year contract he signed with the Sox looks like a much better deal now than it did in 2015.

Two days after Porcello was announced as the Cy Young winner, the Most Valuable Player Awards were given out. Mookie Betts, Mike Trout, center fielder of the Los Angeles Angels and Jose Altuve, second baseman of the Houston Astros were the finalists.

Betts was obviously the Red Sox fans favorite to win the Award. Trout's Angels had finished in fourth place, despite his having had a great year and, although the team's success or failure is not supposed to be a factor, most MVP's have come from teams that have had successful seasons.

Betts had hit .328 with a .534 slugging percentage, had 214 hits, 31 home runs, scored 122 runs and had 26 stolen bases. Perhaps the statistic that best exemplifies his excellent year is the fact that he drove in 113 runs despite hitting in the lead off spot for 109 games of the season.

Despite those numbers and the defense and intangibles he brings to the game, Mookie finished second in the balloting, in one of the closest races ever, to Mike Trout, who won his second MVP in three years. In five years in baseball he has either won the Award or finished second in the voting every year.

Red Sox fans were disappointed that Mookie did not win the 12th Award in Sox history. Previous Sox winners were Tris Speaker, 1912, Jimmie Foxx, 1938, Ted Williams, 1940 and 1949, Jackie Jensen, 1958, Carl Yastrzemski, 1967, Fred Lynn, 1975, Jim Rice, 1978, Roger Clemens, 1986, Mo Vaughn, 1995 and Dustin Pedroia, 2008.

There is every reason to believe that Mookie will continue to put up the type numbers he put up this year and will be an offensive force for the Sox for many years.

With literally everybody, except David Ortiz, coming back and most key players locked into long term commitments to Boston, this team could turn baseball upside down and join the Cubs in dominating baseball for the next several years.

What a year offensively!! Three players with 30 or more homers, five with 25 or more and seven with 15 or more. Three with 100 or more RBI's, seven with 70 or more. 861 runs scored and a team batting average of .282, both marks the best in all of baseball. The highest On Base Percentage, .348 and Slugging Percentage, .461, in all of baseball. The most hits, 1,598 and doubles, 343, in all of baseball.

A year of special performances by the pitchers. A pitcher, Rick Porcello, with 22 wins and just 4 losses, only one at home all year. A former Cy Young Award Winner, David Price, who slipped(?) to 17-9, if you can call 17-9 slipped, and is sure to get better. A 32 year old knuckleballer, Steven Wright who, before his injury in early August caused him to miss the last two months of the season, was 13-5 with a 3.01 ERA.

Despite the collapse in the last week of the season and the first round of the Playoffs, this was the second best team in all of baseball in 2016 and there is no reason to believe that they won't get better. Most of the key position players, Betts, Bogaerts, Bradley, Holt, Vazquez, Holt, Benintendi, Shaw, Moncada and others are young players just beginning to grow into their Major League careers. No one can expect Sandy Leon to have a start like last year but either he or Holiday will be a good back up for Vazquez behind the plate.

The veteran position players, Pedroia, Ramirez, Young and company have been inspired by the ability of the youngsters and still have plenty left in their tanks for the near future And who knows which Pablo Sandoval will show up this year. If he is committed to being a productive member of this team, he has the ability to be a major asset at third or DH.

And, what about DH, now that David is gone? How do you replace a 40 year old designated hitter who hit .315, with 38 homers and 127 RBI's, led the league in doubles with 48 and slugging percentage with .620, finished second in RBI's with 127, third in On Base Percentage with .401 and sixth in batting average at .315?

You have to have faith that Dave Dombrowski will spring for a top notch DH, perhaps even Edward Encarnacion or Joey Bautista, from Toronto, who are both Free Agents, while you pray he doesn't trade away any of his youngsters to acquire someone else. Not to belittle David Ortiz's fantastic swan song but, even without his hitting, the Sox would still have had the highest batting average in all of baseball and they do have hitters who might step into that role if Dombrowski is unable to come up with a replacement.

Youngster Sam Travis, a 23 year old first baseman, who hit .272 at Pawtucket in 49 games before an ACL injury cost him the rest of the season and who had hit .469 with 15 hits in 32 at bats in

Spring Training last year could change the Sox thinking about the DH situation if he has a good spring.

The pitching staff, with Porcello, who no one expects to have another 2016, but who can be expected to be among the best in the league; Price, who you know will get better; Wright, who should come back strong after his long rest; Rodriguez, who, if he lives up to his potential, could be a major factor; Kelly, with his power arm and his strong finish last year, can either start or relieve; Pomeranz, who started 30 games last year between San Diego and Boston with a 3.32 ERA, and even Buchholz, who made a comeback at the end of the year after a stint in the bullpen, could be among the best in baseball. Don't forget Henry Owens, Brian Johnson and a few others possible starters are honing their skills in Pawtucket and Portland as well and are always available on short notice to fill in.

The bullpen, with Kimbrel, a young Closer who throws over 100 and will gain more command and be more effective, Smith, back from surgery and proven capable of being an effective reliever, Barnes, Hembree, Ross, young Robby Scott and the rest will be strong. Tazawa, Uehara and Ziegler have chosen to test the Free Agent Market but any or all of the three could be back and could make a big difference in the bullpen.

The Coaching Staff will all be back, with one major exception, the Bench Coach, Torey Lovullo, who did such a great job in Farrell's absence last year, became Manager of the Arizona Diamondbacks on November 4. This was no surprise. With Farrell coming back as Manager, Lovullo, with his talent, was expected to move on. He was well respected with the team and had developed a special rapport with the players, particularly the younger ones.

He was replaced with Gary Di Sarcina, a twelve year playing veteran who was no stranger to the Red Sox organization. He had coached and Managed at the Red Sox affiliate in Lowell and Managed the Pawtucket Red Sox in 2013.

He also played with John Farrell with the Los Angeles Angels in 1993 and 1994. He played his entire 12 year career with the Anels as a shortstop and had a career batting average of .258 and was named to the All Star team in 1.995

He is a smart baseball man who has the advantage of being familiar with many of the younger Red Sox players who played for him in Pawtucket.

With all this talent and who knows what Dombrowski might add over the winter, Spring Training with this group at Jet Blue Park will be interesting in the coming year. So much talent and so few positions. If you think they had fun playing and were fun and exciting to watch this year, remember the old Red Sox motto 'Wait Til Next Year'. This team will definitely be worth waiting for.